Healing Devotions

DAILY MEDITATIONS AND PRAYERS
BASED ON SCRIPTURES AND HYMNS

BY

ANNE S. WHITE

MOREHOUSE-BARLOW COMPANY :: NEW YORK

Copyright © 1975
by Morehouse-Barlow Co., Inc.
14 East 41st Street
New York, New York 10017

ISBN 8192-1192-3

Library of Congress Catalog Card Number: 75-5218

PRINTED IN THE UNITED STATES OF AMERICA

To my husband, Dick, now in Glory,
in thanksgiving for his
understanding love and cooperation
and
to those who seek healing and wholeness
through its continuous daily devotions,
this book is lovingly dedicated.

Acknowledgements

I wish to express grateful thanks to Zelle Washburn and Laura Candler, prayer-partners and coworkers, whose constructive advice, perspective, and loving support contributed much to the completion of this book.

Thanks also to the Rev. Mr. George Bennett for permission to use some devotionals previously printed in England in *The Healer*, formerly the magazine of the Divine Healing Mission.

I wish to thank proprietors of *The Hymnal of the Protestant Episcopal Church* (U.S.A.); *The Methodist Hymnal; Gospel Melodies* (Baptist Sunday School Board); *Hymns Ancient & Modern* (England); and Oxford University Press, for their cooperation in permissions.

Most Scripture passages quoted are from the Revised Standard Version except where specifically noted (NEB) in the text — indicating they were taken from the New English Bible and quoted with permission of the Oxford University Press and the Cambridge University Press, London. Permission to use the Revised Standard Version of the Bible, copyrighted 1946 and 1952 was granted by the Division of Christian Education, National Council of Churches.

Although most of the hymns referred to are in the public domain, the following persons or organizations kindly gave permission to use the hymns as noted in the pages below.

Clowes & Sons, publishers of *Hymns Ancient & Modern*, used by permission of the proprietors:
"God of mercy, God of grace" by H. F. Lyte, p. 38.
"We are soldiers of Christ, Who is mighty to save" by T. B. Pollock, p. 71.
"Thou to Whom the sick and dying" by G. Thring, p. 68.
"Alleluia! Alleluia! Alleluia! The strife is o'er, the battle done" by F. Pott, p. 66.

Hope Publishing Company:
"Have Thine Own Way, Lord" by Adelaide Pollard, p. 57.

Houghton Mifflin Company:
"Once to every man and nation" by J. R. Lowell, p. 54.
"Dear Lord and Father of mankind" by J. G. Whittier, p. 80.
"All things are thine; no gift have we" by J. G. Whittier, p. 37

Oxford University Press, from *Enlarged Songs of Praise*:
"My God, I love Thee; not because" adpt. by P. Dearmer (1867-1936), p. 38.
"Come risen Lord" by G. W. Briggs (1875-1959), p. 82.

The Parish Press:
"Eternal Father, strong to save" by William Whiting, 1860, p. 71.

The Presbyterian Outlook, Richmond, Virginia; and Ernest Merrill (son):
"Rise up, O men of God" by William P. Merrill, p. 53.

Fleming H. Revell Company:
"O Master, let me walk with thee" by Washington Gladden, p. 56.
"Thine arm, O Lord, in days of old" by E. H. Plumptre, p. 80.
"What a friend we have in Jesus" by Joseph Scriven, p. 76.

The Rodeheaver Co.:
"In the Garden" by C. Austin Miles, p. 76.

Charles Scribner's Sons:
"Joyful, joyful, we adore thee" from *Poems of Henry Van Dyke*, p. 37.

FOREWORD

The seed thought for these meditations on hymns and relevant passages of Scripture came to me after hearing Agnes Sanford speak of the dangers of confusing our subconscious minds by singing hymns and parroting Bible passages without *really* meaning them. I too was guilty of this divided attitude: I had been singing and saying things in Church without taking them literally to heart! In one of my subsequent quiet times, the Lord showed me that this was a form of irreverence and hypocrisy that was akin to blasphemy. I was hailing the power of Jesus one minute and acting the next minute as if God were dead! I was a double-minded person but the Holy Spirit graciously reminded me of St. James' epistle: "But let him ask in faith, with no doubting, for he who doubts is like a wave of the sea that is driven and tossed by the wind. For that person must not suppose that a double-minded man, unstable in all his ways, will receive anything from the Lord." *(1: 6-8)* Two-faced follower that I was, I called myself an earnest Christian and was a faithful attender every time the church door opened!

It was then that the Lord laid it on my heart to write these meditations. He showed me that if I sang hymns or snatches of them throughout the day, my subconscious mind would be filled with these uplifting, constructive ideas, instead of the usual down-pull of negative, fearful thoughts. In my private devotions and in worship services, the hymns and Bible became so interrelated that I found myself often jotting down meditations which seemed to come from both of these inspirations. The nudging of the Holy Spirit made it clear that these thoughts were to be shared in the hope that the Lord might bless others through the idea of starting his day "in Song and Scripture" — affirming and praying "flash prayers" throughout the day so that even in the midst of busy-ness, my thoughts would remain centered in him.

"Thine, O Lord, is the greatness, and the power, and the glory, and the victory, and the majesty; for all that is in the heavens and in the earth is thine; thine is the kingdom, O Lord, and thou art exalted as head above all." *(I Chronicles 29: 11)*

Contents

PART 1

Healing Miracles

As I write the first of these meditations, the Sea of Galilee stretches grey-green toward the horizon, rugged mountains rise behind me and, to the left, the gently sloping hillsides are carpeted with white and yellow daisies, scarlet "lilies of the field" (anemones) and long green grass. We have just been blessed in a service of Holy Communion held outdoors on the slope of the Mount of Beatitudes. A road follows the nearer edge of the sea — the road that leads south from Capernaum. It must have been travelled by Jesus many times. In front of me is the place where Peter may have cast his net into the sea on the other side of the boat at Jesus' command and made a huge catch of fish — and became a fisher of men!

Perhaps for some of us these daily devotions will be casting out nets on the other side of the boat — out of the sea of doubt and despair into the waters of faith in the healing miracles of our Lord.

May the blessedness of Your Presence be with each of us as we make together daily this "Holy Land Pilgrimage" Lord. As we pray the daily sentence prayers, may they continuously keep us mindful of You and Your purposes for us. Amen.

MONDAY, FIRST WEEK   St. Luke 4: 16-21 (NEB).

Jesus fulfilled the prophecy of Isaiah in His earthly ministry not only by preaching in the synagogues but also by manifesting God's Will to heal. The Spirit of the Lord anointed Jesus to proclaim the Good News of the Kingdom: ". . . release for prisoners and recovery of sight for the blind; to let the broken victims go free." When we pray for healing for ourselves or for others, we pray to become capable of a maximum vocation to serve Him!

Lord, touch me and make me whole in mind and body, spirit and soul. Touch others for healing through my prayers today. Amen.

TUESDAY, FIRST WEEK   St. Luke 4: 38-39 (NEB).

Again Jesus healed by the power of His spoken Word. The healing of Peter's mother-in-law evoked such a grateful response that "she got up at once and waited on them." Once a young minister took Jesus at His Word and rebuked a friend's fever in faith that the word of authority had still its ancient power—and the man was healed!

Lord Jesus, speak through me Your word of authority that I may be healed and get up to serve You today. Amen.

WEDNESDAY, FIRST WEEK   St. Luke 5: 12-16 (NEB).

In Biblical times leprosy was a disease signifying spiritual as well as physical uncleanness. Its victims were untouchable. By touching the man and saying, "Indeed I will; be clean again," Jesus proclaimed God's Will to make clean and whole this pitiful, diseased man. Jesus sent him to the priest for ceremonial certification of the cure. This is Jesus' answer to: "If it be Thy Will!" He did not piously tell the leper to go on suffering—He healed him!

Lord, speak to me: "I will; be clean again." Amen.

2::*Healing Miracles*

THURSDAY, FIRST WEEK   St. Luke 5: 17-26 (NEB).

Again we see Jesus' power to forgive sin and make whole. Knowing that guilt was paralyzing the man, Jesus forgave his sins, commanded him to stand up, take up his own bed and return home; to accept his responsibilities once more. Apparently Jesus used the faith of the four friends but challenged the paralytic to accept His forgiveness and act upon the healing at once; to respond to its full implications.

Lord, forgive my sins. Help me to respond in faith. Thanks be for friends' prayers! Amen.

FRIDAY, FIRST WEEK   St. Luke 6: 6-11 (NEB).

Jesus knew the wicked designs of the Pharisees but He fearlessly healed, on the Sabbath, the man with the withered arm to prove that God's compassion was not bound by their legalisms. Jesus demanded that the man stand up before the congregation and prove that it was God's Will to do good and to save life. The man's arm was healed in response to the words of authority: "Stretch out your arm."

Lord, Your word is power. Help me to stretch forth my arm in faith. Amen.

SATURDAY, FIRST WEEK   St. Luke 7: 2-10 (NEB).

Again Jesus' word of authority is used in healing. Again it is the faith of the petitioner, the Roman centurion, not of the patient that Jesus used, commenting that He had not found such faith in Israel. The compassion of the man of authority for his servant, his expectancy and humility, evoked Jesus' admiration. He teaches us today to expect healing as our response to His command to His church.

Lord, I am not worthy that You should come under my roof, but speak the word only and I, Your obedient servant, shall be healed. I thank You that in Your mercy, You are healing my friend now. Amen.

MONDAY, SECOND WEEK   St. Luke 7: 11-17 (NEB).

Twice Jesus raised men from the dead not because of His great compassion for the bereaved but to glorify God! He overruled death. He did not talk about God's Will for the widow's son to die. There was no doubt in His mind as He commanded the mother to stop weeping and the son to rise up. All responded: "God has shown his care for his people" —and the news spread like wildfire.

Lord Jesus, we, too, praise your merciful love and power today. Amen.

TUESDAY, SECOND WEEK   St. Luke 8: 26-39 (NEB).

Jesus had cast out devils and restored an insane man to his right mind. Sometimes when Jesus heals, people are afraid to accept Him. Like the Gergesenes, they act in fear instead of joyfully receiving Him into their hearts. They are afraid He may make some real demand on them and change their lives! Material considerations kept the Gergesenes away. Does shyness, pride or unwillingness to sacrifice time and resources stand between us and our Lord's healing power?

Lord, help me to tell what God has done for me. Amen.

WEDNESDAY, SECOND WEEK   St. Luke 8: 43-48 (NEB).

Often we feel we could be healed by touching Jesus' robe like the woman who had hemorrhaged for twelve years. In the sacrament of Holy Communion we receive "the body and blood of our Lord Jesus Christ." We must go in faith. This woman was medically incurable. She had no one to help her. She braved detection and possible rebuke. Do we go to Holy Communion with her courageous expectancy?

Lord, speak to me, "My daughter, you are healed. God is merciful. Go in peace." Amen.

THURSDAY, SECOND WEEK   St. Luke 8: 49-56 (NEB).

Jesus spoke words of life to Jairus when the servant brought news of his child's death. "Do not be afraid—only show faith and she will be well again." Often today a patient in a weakened state is almost suffocated by gloomy thoughts projected by well-meaning but fearful relatives and friends. Jesus took His "prayer group" with Him and sent away the mourners. He commanded the girl to arise and she stood up and even ate something!

Lord, let me be quickened to new life by faith in Your healing power today. Amen.

FRIDAY, SECOND WEEK   St. Luke 9: 37-43 (NEB).

After Jesus and three disciples had experienced the sublime blessing of the Transfiguration, they came back to find the other disciples defeated, unable to cast the demon out of the epileptic boy. After we have reached spiritual heights, God often seems to test the reality of our growth by bringing us great difficulties to overcome. Jesus was able to heal the boy by rebuking the evil spirit because He had spent much time in prayer and self-discipline.

Lord, make me faithful in my prayers, steady in testings, joyous in Your Presence today. Amen.

SATURDAY, SECOND WEEK   St. Luke 11: 14-26 (NEB).

Jesus healed the man who could not speak by driving out the "devil which was dumb." The man had probably experienced a severe shock of paralyzing fear which Satan had used to bind him. St. Luke the physician seems preoccupied with healings of demon possession. Like many today, the people were astonished but tried to deprecate the Lord's Power. Jesus clearly showed the connection between the coming of God's Kingdom and the casting out of demons "by the finger of God."

Lord, bring in Your Kingdom in power today. Amen.

MONDAY, THIRD WEEK   St. Luke 13: 10-17 (NEB).

The duration of an illness made no difference to Jesus; though it is often a stumbling block to us. He healed a woman who had been crippled for 18 years. First, He assured her of release and then He laid hands on her. Immediately she straightened up and praised God! As happens today, some objected to Jesus' method of healing but He shamed them and proved His mercy that would not let the woman suffer even one more day.

Lord, set me free today from a crippling of mind, and any spirit of criticism, that is reflected in my body. Amen.

TUESDAY, THIRD WEEK   St. Luke 14: 1-6 (NEB).

The Pharisees were angry because Jesus let nothing stop His healing work, not even their rules about the Sabbath. Today people find equal frustration if they try to legislate the Holy Spirit! He does not abide by manmade conventions nor work on man's schedules. Jesus healed the man of dropsy on the Sabbath at the Pharisee's dinner table. How often God heals unpredictably today, even the unchurched! We must never try to limit the Holy Spirit.

Lord, release Your healing Power as You choose today. Amen.

WEDNESDAY, THIRD WEEK   St. Luke 17: 11-19 (NEB).

Ten men called out for pity but only the despised Samaritan praised God after his healing! Many today ask for prayers but forget to thank God after He heals them. Do we just want to get well or do we want God, by the touch of His love, to make us whole? Holy Communion is a service of thanksgiving: as the priest says, "Preserve thy body and soul," we can be made whole, in mind, spirit, body and soul.

Lord, thanks be that I am made whole. Amen.

THURSDAY, THIRD WEEK   St. Luke 18: 35-43 (NEB).

Blind people are piteously numerous in Jerusalem and Jericho today. Our Lord had special compassion for them. This man who was annoyingly persistent was rebuked by the people but his spiritual sight was greater than theirs. He recognized Jesus as "Son of David." Bartimaeus knew what he wanted and persisted in faith till Jesus spoke words of healing that he might receive his sight; his praise of God was contagious! Is ours?

Lord, that I may receive my sight, spiritual and mental as well as physical. Amen.

FRIDAY, THIRD WEEK   St. Luke 22: 50-51 (NEB).

Jesus healed the ear of the High Priest's servant who had come to help arrest Him. In anger over Judas' betrayal, one disciple had acted without love but Jesus quickly repaired the damage with His healing touch. Only Jesus could show such mercy in time of turmoil! He reacted in love and compassion when others acted in hate and treachery. Can we claim to be *His followers?*

Lord, heal me of my hasty judgments and teach me to act always in Your perfect love. Amen.

SATURDAY, THIRD WEEK   St. John 4: 46-54 (NEB).

Jesus spoke with such authority that the father believed His words and started home—acting in faith on this belief. Do we act in faith today, moving in response to the healing promises of Jesus? Having gone part way, the father found his faith. His expectancy had been justified. Servants brought good news: "Your boy is going to live." The father did not say, "What a coincidence!" He noted that his son was healed at the *exact* hour, and he became a believer!

Lord, I claim, I act upon Your healing promises now. I go in faith, believing. Amen.

MONDAY, FOURTH WEEK   St. John 5: 2-18 (NEB).

Many had been healed at the pool of Bethesda. One man who had been crippled for 38 years attracted Jesus who challenged his will to recover and commanded him to rise and walk in faith. Jesus saw his deeper need; obedience made healing possible. Later Jesus commanded, ". . . leave your sinful ways, or you may suffer something worse." Was his sin self-pity, putting blame on others, adverse conditions, etc.? Do we *really* want to accept the old responsibilities of being well and give up coddling?

Lord, forgive me; I have had excuses, not faith. Amen.

TUESDAY, FOURTH WEEK   St. John 9: 1-41 (NEB).

Not all illness is the result of personal sin, Jesus declared. He spread a saliva "ointment" on the eyes of the man born blind. The man responded in faith to Christ's command to wash in the pool and was healed at Siloam. Later, he bravely faced banishment from the synagogue as he witnessed to the glory of God whose power had been manifested. Jesus revealed His true identity to the man.

Lord, I believe, I praise, I worship You. Amen.

WEDNESDAY, FOURTH WEEK   St. John 11: 1-44 (NEB).

Before the stone was removed from Lazarus' tomb, Jesus said significantly, "Did I not tell you that if you have faith you will see the glory of God?" Then He prayed, "Father, I thank thee: thou hast heard me . . . Lazarus, come forth." Jesus expected God to hear and answer His prayer: the Father would be glorified in the Son's work, therefore He had the authority to command the dead to rise! Do we, today, pray with Jesus' expectancy, faith, authority?

Father, I thank You. I am healed! Amen.

THURSDAY, FOURTH WEEK   St. Mark 7: 24-30 (NEB).
Jesus tested the Syro-Phoenician woman's faith by putting
obstacles to test her humility before answering her prayers.
She did not become resentful but patiently and persistently
held her prayer up to Him, trusting His mercy and loving
justice as well as His Power. So often we become rebellious
instead of humble when our prayers are not quickly answered. She accepted His promises *before* she saw the answer.
She went home to find her faith had been rewarded!

Lord, forgive my impatience; I await Your answer. Amen.

FRIDAY, FOURTH WEEK   St. Mark 7: 32-37 (NEB).
The people were greatly astonished because Jesus healed
instantly the deaf and dumb man. Again Jesus took the man
away from the crowd and again He used saliva and the word
of authority in His healing. It was impossible to suppress this
good news of the man who brought such blessings. How
many long for the Good News that Jesus is the same, yester-
day, today and forever! He still says "Be opened" and the
deaf hear.

Lord, open my spiritual ears to hear Your voice: "Ephpha-
tha." Amen.

SATURDAY, FOURTH WEEK   St. Mark 8: 22-26 (NEB).
At Bethsaida people brought a blind man begging Jesus to
touch him. Our Lord led the man away from the crowd.
Using spittle as an ointment, Jesus laid His hands on the
man's eyes; his sight was partially restored. To complete the
healing, Jesus again laid on hands and the man had his vision
clearly restored. More than one laying-on of hands may be
necessary to complete our Lord's healing through imperfect
channels today.

Lord, restore my sight. I praise You in advance. Amen.

MONDAY, FIFTH WEEK   St. Matthew 9: 27-31 (NEB).

Two blind men cried out for pity and Jesus challenged them to state their faith publicly. Then He said, touching their eyes, "As you have believed, so let it be." Their faith *preceded* their healing. They had heard of Jesus' healings and now as they acknowledged Him as "Son of David" they followed Him, not waiting for someone to bring Him to them. Jesus of Nazareth is passing by. Will you believe in His touch through His Church today?

Son of David, Jesus, I believe; have mercy on me. Amen.

TUESDAY, FIFTH WEEK   St. Matthew 9: 32-34 (NEB).

Demonic possession was prevalent in Jesus' day. In this case the devil controlling the man's tongue prevented him from speaking. Jesus, with perfect discernment, recognized the devil and cast it out of the victim who began to talk. The amazed crowd exclaimed that nothing like this had happened before. Their local magic-workers had no such power as that of Jesus who proclaimed God's Kingdom not only in words but in deeds. Do we?

Lord, help us proclaim Your Kingdom in healing love. Amen.

WEDNESDAY, FIFTH WEEK   St. Luke 4: 40-41 (NEB).

Even demons possessing the mentally deranged people of Jesus' day were aware that He was "the Son of God," the Messiah. Face to face with Jesus, these pitiable victims of demonic possession were set free as the Lord rebuked the devils. The power of our Lord was greater than the power of Satan. Do we really believe this today? Do we claim it? Friends of the sick brought them to Jesus. He patiently laid hands on them, healing them one by one.

Lord, Jesus, we bring You . . . (name) . . . on the stretcher of prayer for healing. Amen.

THURSDAY, FIFTH WEEK   St. Matthew 9: 35-36 (NEB).

St. Matthew describes Jesus' three-fold ministry as "teaching in their synagogues, announcing the good news of the Kingdom, and curing every kind of ailment and disease. The sight of the people moved him to pity: they were like sheep without a shepherd, harassed and helpless." Jesus' miracles were performed out of compassion and for the purpose of glorifying God. He did not heal to attract attention as a spectacular gimmick; He healed of His Father's love.

Thank You, Father, Your love is healing me now. Amen.

FRIDAY, FIFTH WEEK   St. Luke 6: 17-19 (NEB).

After calling the disciples, Jesus came down from the hills to find crowds from Jerusalem, Judea, Tyre and Sidon. They "had come to listen to him, and to be cured of their diseases." Everyone felt the power that went out from Him and tried to touch Him. He healed all. Today through the members of His Body the Church, Christ can still heal; but we need the faith of the *whole* Church behind the finger that touches in His Name!

Thank you, Lord. Your touch is healing me now. Amen.

SATURDAY, FIFTH WEEK   St. Luke 7: 18-23 (NEB).

Jesus replied to John's sincere question about His Messiahship by healing "many sufferers from diseases, plagues, and evil spirits; and on many blind people he bestowed sight." Then He turned to John's disciples, specifically charging them to tell John what they had seen and heard. The proof of His Sonship was in the healing works by which Jesus glorified the Father. Prophetically He said, "Happy is the man who does not find me a stumbling-block."

Jesus, use me to tell others of Your healing power. Amen.

MONDAY, SIXTH WEEK   St. Luke 9: 1-2; 10-11 (NEB).

The apostles had been sent out by Jesus with "power and authority to overcome all the devils and to cure diseases . . . to proclaim the Kingdom of God and to heal." They had told the good news and healed the sick everywhere. On their return, Jesus took them to Bethsaida for further teaching but the crowds discovered the place and followed Him. He was not angry with their persistency; He welcomed them, spoke to them of God's Kingdom and cured all those needing healing.

Lord, bring Your Kingdom into my heart today. Amen.

TUESDAY, SIXTH WEEK   St. Mark 6: 53-56 (NEB).

If Jesus appeared visibly in our churches today, would we have "scoured that whole country-side" bringing "the sick on stretchers to any place where he was reported to be?" These people had faith and compassion enough to lay their sick in the marketplaces begging Jesus "to let them simply touch the edge of his cloak; and all who touched him were cured." Would we have their faith or would we, as at Nazareth, try to shove Him over a precipice?

Lord, forgive our faithlessness in Your church today. Amen.

WEDNESDAY, SIXTH WEEK St. Matthew 15: 29-31 (NEB).

This is being written on perhaps the same hillside overlooking the Sea of Galilee. Imagine the procession of simple, awe-struck people, crowds jostling to bring blind, dumb, and crippled folk before this wonderful Man should leave their neighborhood. Imagine their amazement and joy as the lame walked, the blind saw and the dumb spoke! Would we give "praise to the God of Israel," or would we call Jesus a crackpot? What of those He heals today?

Lord, I see You as the Great Physician still. Amen.

THURSDAY, SIXTH WEEK
St. Matthew 19: 1-2;
St. Luke 5: 15-16 (NEB).

Whether He was in Galilee or Judea across the Jordan, great crowds followed Jesus and He healed them. There are still some people who object to healing services but our Lord did not disperse the crowds saying, "You can be healed only through a personal interview with a private laying-on of hands." He healed them all. But "from time to time he would withdraw to lonely places for prayer." The healing ministry must spring from much consecrated prayer.

Lord, bless my "quiet time." Make me a better channel of faith and love for others. Amen.

FRIDAY, SIXTH WEEK
St. Matthew 21: 12-15 (NEB).

Jesus drove out money-changers and vendors of pigeons and animals saying they were making the temple into a "robbers' cave." As authority He quoted Scripture: "My house shall be called a house of prayer." Immediately afterwards blind men and cripples came to Jesus, and He healed them, to the indignation of chief priests and doctors of law. Prayer and healing of the sick are God's business! Are we too busy for His business today?

Lord, forgive our blindness to Your healing Will today. Amen.

SATURDAY, SIXTH WEEK
St. Mark 6: 1-6 (NEB).

Nazareth reminds us of the world today because of its attitude of doubt and unbelief. Even Jesus was "taken aback by their want of faith!" Even Jesus "could work no miracle there, except that he put his hands on a few sick people and healed them." Even Jesus found doubt "among his kinsmen and family." This lack of faith is part of the sin of the world. It is a wonder that God can heal today because of the world's want of faith!

Lord, forgive our sin of lack of faith. Amen.

Daily Devotions::13

MONDAY, SEVENTH WEEK   St. Luke 9: 1-6;
St. Mark 6: 12-13 (NEB).

All three synoptic gospels record Jesus' commission to the disciples. He "gave them power and authority to overcome all the devils and to cure diseases, and sent them to proclaim the kingdom of God and to heal." St. Matthew names the apostles proclaiming this message. St. Mark reports that they ". . . called publicly for repentance. They drove out many devils, and many sick people they anointed with oil and cured." The apostles went out in obedience to Jesus' commission and healed the sick.

Lord, increase our faith to obey You: as the disciples did! Amen.

TUESDAY, SEVENTH WEEK   St. Luke 10: 1-20 (NEB).

St. Luke the Physician records the sending out of the seventy-two also: "heal the sick there, and say, 'The kingdom of God has come close to you.' " They returned jubilantly: " 'In your name, Lord,' they said, 'even the devils submit to us'." Healing was the other half of the proclaiming of the Kingdom of God: not an end in itself, as is misunderstood sometimes today. Accepting the Kingship of Christ in our hearts is the end achieved by preaching and healing—two phases of His work.

Lord, rule in my heart today; make me Your kingdom. Amen.

WEDNESDAY, SEVENTH WEEK
St. Matthew 4: 23-25 (NEB).

St. Matthew pictures Jesus' ministry thus: ". . . teaching in the synagogues, preaching the gospel of the Kingdom, and curing whatever illness or infirmity there was among the people." This is the Gospel Jesus commanded us to proclaim through His Body, the Church, today. Healing was a definite part of His Gospel, along with teaching and preaching. Why do we default on healing? Crowds came from Galilee, the Decapolis, Jerusalem, all Judea and even Transjordan and He healed all.

Lord, proclaim through us the Kingdom. Amen.

THURSDAY, SEVENTH WEEK   Acts 3: 1-16 (NEB).

After Pentecost, Peter preached and healed. Today, healing should follow preaching of repentance and acceptance of Christ's forgiveness of sin and of the gift of the Holy Spirit. Peter claimed nothing of or for himself: "the Name of Jesus, by awakening faith, has strengthened this man, whom you see and know, and this faith has made him completely well." In the Name of Jesus, His Body the Church can increase the faith of the sick to be healed.

Lord, quicken the faith of Your Church to heal in Your Name today. Amen.

FRIDAY, SEVENTH WEEK   Acts 9: 10-19;
                                              22: 11-13 (NEB).

Those who speak of St. Paul's "thorn in the flesh" (as proof that God does not will bodily healing) forget that Jesus healed St. Paul of his physical blindness through the laying-on of Ananias' hands. He courageously obeyed the Lord's command although Saul had ruthlessly persecuted Christians. As Ananias laid his hands on Saul, the "scales fell from his eyes, and he regained his sight. Thereupon he was baptized . . . and his strength returned."

Lord, let the scales of pride, prejudice, resentment fall from my eyes; heal me to Your glory in my soul. Amen.

SATURDAY, SEVENTH WEEK   Acts 9: 32-35 (NEB).

Peter said confidently to Aeneas, a bed-ridden paralytic for eight years: "Jesus Christ cures you; get up and make your bed." What if Aeneas had said, "Oh, I'm afraid I'll fall" or

"Does this mean I must take my full share of responsibilities now?" Jesus demanded a response of faith. The sick had to act upon His words and, in the *doing,* their healing was manifested! Do we *act as if* we are healed after the prayer for healing?

Lord, I now accept the full consequences of my healing. Thanks be I am healed! Amen.

MONDAY, EIGHTH WEEK   Acts 9: 36-42 (NEB).

Peter was there when Jesus raised Jairus' daughter from the dead. Like Jesus, Peter sent the mourners out before he prayed. He then said, "Tabitha, arise." He had received the Lord's authority to raise the dead and he acted upon it in faith. The woman opened her eyes and Peter helped her to stand. "Many came to believe in the Lord" as they saw with their own eyes His healing power, the same as in His earthly ministry, working through one of His apostles.

Lord, increase my faith to act upon Your healing words now. Amen.

TUESDAY, EIGHTH WEEK   Acts 10: 38 (NEB).

Peter, preaching to Cornelius, proclaimed Jesus whom "God anointed . . . with the Holy Spirit and with power. He went about doing good and healing all who were oppressed by the devil, for God was with him." Peter clearly stated that Jesus healed because God was *with Him* and because the sick were oppressed by the devil. Why do many foolishly claim sickness to be the Will of God instead of recognizing it as Satan's work? Has God ever changed His Will to heal, or have we lost faith?

Lord, have mercy on our faithlessness today; forgive us. Amen.

WEDNESDAY, EIGHTH WEEK   Acts 14: 8-18 (NEB).

Paul at Lystra felt Jesus' compassion for the crippled and saw "he had the faith to be cured, so he said to him in a loud voice, 'Stand up straight on your feet'; and he sprang up and started to walk." The amazed bystanders, thinking Paul and Barnabas were gods, started to offer sacrifices to them. Today, too, there is danger that the channels for God's healing be exalted: they are "only human beings no less mortal than you."

It is Your power, Lord; glorify Yourself through me. Amen.

THURSDAY, EIGHTH WEEK   Acts 16: 16-18 (NEB).

Spiritism is still practised today. It is very dangerous to attempt contact with spirits of the dead through mediums and seances. The slave girl's psychic powers were exploited by her owners in their fortunetelling business. Paul recognized that a satanic divining spirit possessed her and commanded it to come out of her. The owners, deprived of their wicked way of exploitation, turned in anger on Paul and Silas to have them jailed. Beware of the occult!

Lord, I seek guidance only from You through Your Holy Spirit today. Lead me as You will. Take away from me any desire to dabble in fortunetelling, horoscopes, or ouija boards. Amen.

FRIDAY, EIGHTH WEEK   Acts 20: 7-12 (NEB).

At Troas in an upper room Paul had led the Christian assembly for the breaking of bread (Communion) and had addressed them until midnight. Eutychus fell asleep on the window ledge and dropped two floors to the ground. Paul with confident trust silenced their fear and, acting in faith, revived the boy. How seldom in the hubbub today do we have the courage and faith to say: "Stop this commotion; there is still life in him."

Lord Jesus, silence my fears; increase my faith today. Amen.

SATURDAY, EIGHTH WEEK   Acts 28: 3-6 (NEB).

When shipwrecked at Malta, Paul was treated kindly by the islanders until a snake fastened on his hand. Superstitiously people thought Paul was a murderer escaping from divine justice. But Paul was unharmed and shook the snake off into the fire. Then the islanders decided Paul was a god. We, too, make "gods" out of people today who are a channel for the Holy Spirit. Instead we must realize that the Holy Spirit can use even "a broken straw" if we are empty enough of self.

Lord, fill me with Your Holy Spirit; protect me from evil; use me as You will. Amen.

MONDAY, NINTH WEEK   Acts 28: 7-9 (NEB).

While at Malta, Paul was entertained by the chief magistrate, Publius, whose father had a recurring illness. "Paul . . . after prayer, laid his hands upon him and healed him; whereupon the other sick people on the island came also and were cured." St. Paul's "thorn in the flesh" did not stop his faith in God's Will and power to heal—indeed he thus *manifested God's Will!* Why do people hide behind this "thorn" when their faith is weak today? Paul didn't!

Lord, I am weak but You are abundantly able. Heal me that I may better help others. Amen.

TUESDAY, NINTH WEEK   Acts 5: 12-16 (NEB).

Because Peter and other apostles used to meet with the people at Solomon's Cloister, it became customary to bring the sick and demon-possessed there from all the towns around Jerusalem, and to leave them on beds and stretchers so that Peter's shadow might fall on them as he passed by. Peter the coward was transformed by the Holy Spirit at Pentecost into a man of such great faith that being in his presence meant healing. He was a channel to bring Jesus' Presence to the sick!

Lord, Your Presence is real. You are healing me now. Amen.

WEDNESDAY, NINTH WEEK Acts 14: 3; 8: 8; 6: 8 (NEB).

Paul and Barnabas at Iconium, Stephen at Jerusalem, Philip in Samaria were all used by the Lord to proclaim boldly God's Kingdom ". . . and he confirmed the message of his grace by causing signs and miracles to be worked at their hands." "Paralysed and crippled folk were cured; and there was great joy in that city." These apostles were "full of grace and power." They did not stop to count the cost. Do we? They relied on the Lord to fulfill *His promises.*

Lord, use my faith as Your channel to bless others today; lead me to those in need. Amen.

THURSDAY, NINTH WEEK Acts 2: 42-43; 5: 40-42 (NEB).

The apostles were ordinary men when they were called; they became extraordinary men because they kept their promises to follow Jesus—through His Resurrection experience, on to Pentecost! They prayed and received the full anointing of the Holy Spirit to carry on His work, even at the cost of their lives! Christ Jesus lived within them, empowering and guiding them. Are we fulfilling our baptismal vows to follow Him? Is He *really* our Lord and Master? Is He our personal Saviour?

My Lord, I praise You, I proclaim You, Saviour, Healer, Redeemer. Amen.

FRIDAY, NINTH WEEK   St. Matthew 8: 16-17.

Although when at the altar we may not see Jesus physically as the sick come for the laying-on of hands today, we can know and feel Christ's Presence. As He came that evening in Capernaum and "healed all who were sick," He was fulfilling Isaiah's prophecy: "He took our infirmities and bore our diseases." He still comes to the sad, the physically and mentally ill, those who have ignored Him out of ignorance or wilfulness. His searching eyes penetrate our hearts to show us the very "skeletons in the closet" we have tried hardest to hide!

Lord Jesus, who healed the sick in Your earthly ministry, show me if some secret fear or resentment is causing my illness, poisoning my body as it poisons my mind and soul. Touch me, heal me with Your ancient power. Amen.

SATURDAY, NINTH WEEK   St. Luke 4: 31-37 (NEB).

Jesus used His authority to cast out the evil spirit that possessed the man in the synagogue in Capernaum. In China and India, in England and America, demons have been cast out in the Name and authority of Jesus Christ. A spirit of hate or fear, deceit or jealousy can possess a person making him "mentally ill." Such soul-sickness responds today to Jesus' command made in faith by one of His consecrated servants—when the person is willing!

Lord Jesus, command the demons of hate, fear, deceit and jealousy to come out of those today who need Your healing word of authority to set them free. Amen.

PART 2

Hymns of Praise
and Thanksgiving

In these next three sections we shall meditate daily on a hymn that seems to accentuate our passage of Scripture. If, while doing routine chores, we sing parts of the hymn throughout the day, we shall implant their helpful thoughts in our subconscious minds and lift our spirits to meet the challenges with our Lord's Power, not just our feeble strength alone. Reinforcement of Scripture by singing hymns makes us more aware of the deeper implications of both. When we sing the hymns on Sunday at church they will have more meaning to us because of our meditations during the week. We need not have fine voices to sing while we are about our tasks—we need only be willing "to make a joyful noise unto the Lord." Our first section is on praise and thanksgiving for this is the best place to start God's day—expressing our love for our Lord in praise of Him!

Heavenly Father, we praise You for giving us victory through our Lord and Saviour, Jesus Christ. Make us more open to accept all that is available to us in Him and through the Holy Spirit. We praise You—Father, Son and Holy Spirit —not only in words but in daily living. Amen.

MONDAY, TENTH WEEK   Acts 3: 6 (NEB).

"All hail the power of Jesus' Name"

Peter and John called to a cripple: "I have no silver or gold; but what I have I give you: in the name of Jesus Christ of Nazareth, walk." We sing of the power of Jesus' Name—but do we really believe as they obviously did? Are these just words?: "Hail him who saves you by his grace/And crown him Lord of all." As we pray in His Name do we ask *to be made into His nature*? Sickness gives time to ponder our *true* needs. Then He can heal us.

Jesus, make the power of Your Name real to me today. Amen.

TUESDAY, TENTH WEEK   Hebrews 13: 14-16 (NEB).

"Alleluia! sing to Jesus"

Do we "Through Jesus . . . continually offer up to God the sacrifice of praise?" A busy minister has a printed card on his desk: "Praise Him, anyway!" Are we able to sing this hymn of praise on "dry" days when the reality of our faith ebbs? If so, we shall find the tide turned—our feelings will begin to change as our thoughts center on Jesus, not our problem! We sing: ". . . his the triumph/His the victory alone." But at the first sign of pain we often lose faith!

Jesus, keep my faith praising You—not claiming my ailments. Amen.

WEDNESDAY, TENTH WEEK   Revelation 21: 1-4.

"Glorious things of thee are spoken"

We are cheered by thoughts of the city of God where "streams of living waters,/Springing from eternal love" make healing a fore-gone conclusion. In Christ we look to the future with joyous anticipation; we are members of the City of God through the grace of our Lord. It doesn't matter what the world thinks, for all its pleasures and boasts will fade.

When we suddenly become aware of the transitoriness of life through illness or death, we are comforted to know that we come from God and we return to Him!

Thank You, Lord, that I am a citizen of heaven. Amen.

THURSDAY, TENTH WEEK St. John 15: 11.
"Love divine, all loves excelling"

When our hearts are filled with "love divine" Christ can give us His joy—even in the midst of pain or trouble. He promised us this and He always keeps His promises: it is we who break the conditions of *abiding* in His love, of giving out His love to others no matter what the situation. We are (as our hymn says) to "Pray, and praise thee, without ceasing,/Glory in thy perfect love." We are to "*glance* at the problems and *gaze* at Jesus."

Lord, "Finish then thy new creation" in . . (name) . . and in me. Keep me loving, lifting them to You. Amen.

FRIDAY, TENTH WEEK Philippians 4: 6-7.
"Now thank we all our God"

St. Paul wrote: ". . . in everything by prayer and supplication with thanksgiving let your requests be made known to God." But are we *really* thankful? Are we thanking Him for *His Presence,* or bewailing our difficulties? Do we thank Him "With heart, and hands, and voices,/Who wondrous things hath done"? Or have we, like the Israelites, quickly forgotten past deliverances? He alone can "guide us when perplext,/ And free us from all ills in this world and the next."

Thank You, Father. Forgive my preoccupation with my problems, my ingratitude. Amen.

SATURDAY, TENTH WEEK St. Luke 24: 33-43.
"Come, ye faithful, raise the strain"

The Resurrection was no myth, no imaginary tale promoted by the followers of Jesus! It was a soul-shaking fact, attested to by hundreds who saw Jesus afterwards—those who ate with Him on the beach, or walked the road to Emmaus with Him. God had raised Jesus from the dead so that we, by believing in Him, might be saved! No wonder early Christians used the favorite salutation, "The Lord is risen!"

Lord Jesus, You won for us the victory over sin on the first Good Friday. Let every day be a true Resurrection experience. Amen.

MONDAY, ELEVENTH WEEK   St. John 12: 13; 19: 6; and St. Matthew 25: 40.

"All glory, laud, and honor"

How guilty are we who sing "Hosanna" on Sunday and by Friday have nailed Jesus to the Cross with hatred for our fellow humans! He said: ". . . as you did it to one of the least of these my brethren, you did it to me." He accepts our prayers and anthems—even though He knows full well that we shall also shout "Crucify Him" when He makes some demand that means giving up our differences with our brethren!

Lord, give us a real sense of Your mercy, that we praise You not only with words, but in our lives of self-giving love. Amen.

TUESDAY, ELEVENTH WEEK   Revelation 4: 8.

"Holy, Holy, Holy! Lord God Almighty"

Our hymn is of adoration. Those whose eyes are blinded so that they do not "see" God may disparage Him as if their failure to acknowledge Him had some power to deny His existence! God never changes. He is the ". . . Lord God Almighty, who was and is and is to come!" He is both merciful and mighty. All the wonders of His creation only bear witness to the praise that is His due. "The God of the Infinite is also God of the infinitesimal" but our finite minds are slow to comprehend this.

Thank You for being Almighty God and my loving Heavenly Father also. Amen.

WEDNESDAY, ELEVENTH WEEK   Philippians 3: 8-10.
"When I survey the wondrous cross"

Into the stillness of our hearts—satiated with possessions, or torn with anguish over broken relationships or imprisoned by fears—He comes, the Prince of Glory who stooped to die for you and me! Battered, bruised, bloody, a crown of thorns upon His head—He experienced all this for us! What have we done to deserve this Grace? Nothing! It is unmerited. I cannot earn it but I can respond with thanksgiving. "Love so amazing, so divine,/Demands my soul, my life, my all."

Thank You for saving my soul and making me whole, Lord. Thank You for Your love that meets me in my greatest need to lose self in You. Amen.

THURSDAY, ELEVENTH WEEK   Psalm 103.
"Praise, my soul, the King of heaven"

If more Christians were truly accepting the truth of today's hymn and Scripture, there would be much less illness. "Ransomed, healed, restored, forgiven,/Evermore his praises sing." Jesus, the Great Physician, has done for us already what you and I need. Peace of mind comes *if* we accept His forgiveness and forgive ourselves and others as He has already forgiven us. Does some unrepented sin stand between us and the Lord? He has already forgiven all our sins and will heal all our diseases.

Jesus, help me now to forgive myself and any who have ever hurt me. I need Your help for I cannot do it alone. Amen.

FRIDAY, ELEVENTH WEEK   Acts 1: 7-8.

"Come, thou almighty King"

The anonymous author of this hymn realizes what we often do not: that we need to ask God's help even to sing His praises! We are created to be dependent on Him but our pride keeps us struggling against such dependence. We cannot conceive of the magnitude of God's love and power; but we can ask for the Holy Spirit to lead us into all truth and *give us His power* to witness to the glory of the Father. We can humbly ask Jesus, the Incarnate Word, to establish *His* healing righteousness in and through us.

Father, Son and Holy Spirit—blessed Trinity of love—we praise You now and evermore. Amen.

SATURDAY, ELEVENTH WEEK   Psalm 121: 1-2.

"God of our fathers, whose almighty hand"

In these troubled times this hymn of praise strengthens our faith that God whose almighty hand has led us in the past will continue to be our guide and strengthener against the evils of war and strife which seek to divide us. We need to claim this psalm's promise: "My help comes from the Lord, who made heaven and earth." We need to pray that our God in His justice will show us *how* to work out tensions and bring the true brotherhood of humans—even as He has already brought Christians of different creeds closer together in His divine love.

Lord, dissolve our divisions and break down our partitions in praise of Your love. Amen.

MONDAY, TWELFTH WEEK   Psalm 104: 24, 33.

"O worship the King, all glorious above"

How manifold are the Lord's wonders of creation which even our astronauts extol as they travel to the moon! God created us in wisdom and for our well-being He created the earth upon which we live. The God of the Infinite cares about the details of our lives with a father's love. Our hymn reminds us that He is "Our Maker, Defender, Redeemer, and Friend." We sing gratefully in praise of His power and His compassionate love. If we truly respond to His love, we will not exploit others for our own pleasure but become instruments of His right-use-ness.

Lord, I praise You today as I yield myself to You to be a witness to Your glory. Amen.

TUESDAY, TWELFTH WEEK   Philippians 2: 9-11.
"Jesus, the very thought of thee"

For those who truly know Jesus as their personal Saviour, the very thought of Him stirs up a response of love and praise. His is truly the Name above every name. He is the only One who can bring peace to the guilt-ridden through His forgiving love. In those who seek Him *first* as King of their hearts, there is a peace for which there is no substitute! His love fills the deep hunger of the heart so that we are never alone. No earthly rejection can devastate those who have put Him on the throne.

Thank You, Jesus, for lifting me out of bondage to fear, loneliness, grief and bitterness into the freedom of Your love. Amen.

WEDNESDAY, TWELFTH WEEK   St. Luke 9: 23-27.
"Lead on, O King eternal"

Our battlecry is against sin's devastation in human hearts. Sin is not a popular concept today, but it still exists. Inhumanity is expressed in different ways but it is, nonetheless, sin against God. His Kingdom will come as we follow Him—through acts of mercy and loving kindness, in self-denial overcoming greed, cruelty and selfishness in our world. Healing of bodies follows the healing of minds and spirits and the healing of broken relationships. Jesus came to establish God's Kingdom on earth.

Thank You, Jesus, that Your Kingdom brings gladness, love and peace to our troubled world. Use me today—Your way! Amen.

THURSDAY, TWELFTH WEEK   Romans 6: 12-19; and
Galatians 5: 13.

"'Tis the old-time religion"

"Oldtime religion" versus "new morality" is argued today but Jesus said He came to bring "Life"—His risen Life, a more abundant life—not living by the law. (The Jews had to keep more than 600 laws!) In Christ we live by grace but we are not to *misuse* our freedom as an "opportunity for the flesh, but through love be servants of one another." The "suffering servant" Jesus is the same Christ who lives and will reign on the Judgment Day when His parable of the sheep and goats will be fulfilled. Are we ready for His return?

Thank You, Jesus, for revealing Yourself to men by becoming Man: that we might live by Your grace. Amen.

FRIDAY, TWELFTH WEEK   Acts 4: 8-12; and
St. Matthew 28: 5-10.

"Jesus Christ is risen today"

Easter is a day to sing Alleluia—praise to our heavenly King "Who endured the cross and grave . . ./Sinners to redeem and save!" This suffering was *voluntary* for the Son of God could have called upon legions of angels to deliver Him had He wanted to save Himself. He chose to pay the supreme price, to sacrifice His own life so that by His victory He could redeem *us*. As we claim His Victory over sin, Satan can have no power to bind us in our sins. Each Sunday can be a "little Easter," a day of resurrection and renewal as we join with the company of heaven singing "Alleluia! Jesus Christ is risen."

Praise the Lord whose love redeems me from self-centeredness! Amen.

SATURDAY, TWELFTH WEEK   Psalm 118: 24.

" 'Welcome, happy morning!' age to age shall say"

Do we awaken in this spirit each morning saying: "This is the day which the Lord has made; let us rejoice and be glad in it," or do we groan in dread? A woman was healed of early morning depression by affirming this Scripture as her first thoughts on waking. This "prescription" included singing hymns of praise throughout the day while she did her household chores. As our ancient sixth century Easter hymn promises, she was truly loosed from her prison of despair and discouragement, two of Satan's strongest chains. The Resurrection Life of Jesus flowed into her whole being as she praised Him—at first by faith; and then by sight!

Lord Jesus, be the Author and Finisher of my faith today as I praise Your Victory. Amen.

MONDAY, THIRTEENTH WEEK   Acts 1: 6-8.

"Jesus shall reign where'er the sun"

We are to be His witnesses to the world so that people of every land shall know and praise Jesus. Even the angels of heaven will join in praise and "earth repeat the loud Amen." Endless prayer will be the work of His Kingdom stretching round the world. So wrote Isaac Watts in 1719 as the Church was embarking on her missionary period. Have we grown sluggish in our witness to our healing, redeeming Lord? Do we personally proclaim daily His abiding indwelling peace, love and joy which sets us free from the prison of self?

Thank You, Jesus, that You love and forgive me even when I have been a poor witness to Your glory. Amen.

TUESDAY, THIRTEENTH WEEK   Philippians 1: 12-14.

"Faith of our fathers! living still"

The early Christian martyrs bequeathed to us a priceless heritage of faith and joy that overcame imprisonment, burning at the stake, and death by the sword! Are we bequeathing that kind of faith to our children? Or do they see us breaking down under pressures of modern living, consuming a record-breaking amount of pain-killing tablets, tranquilizers and alcohol? Are we more concerned with our petty aches and pains, or can we forget them in a deeper concern for the ills of mankind? Can we love foe as well as friend and lift both to God in prayers of faith? Do we praise Him *before* we see the answer?

Father, we praise You as God of our fathers who is concerned with our world that needs healing today. Amen.

WEDNESDAY, THIRTEENTH WEEK   Jude 1: 20-21.

"Holy Father, great Creator"

Our Scripture and hymn proclaim the fullness of the Godhead: God the Father whose creation and children we are; God the Son, Jesus, the Lord, our Redeemer; and God the Holy Spirit, our Sanctifier and Comforter, who leads us into all Truth as we pray. Mere human explanations fall short of such a great mystery for we struggle to comprehend the things of faith through the narrow aperture of human intellect. We do not understand fully the mysteries of electricity yet we use it every day to make our lives more complete. We can pray for the world as well as ourselves, in thanksgiving!

Lord, build us up in faith in the Love of God and mercy of our Saviour whom we praise today. Amen.

THURSDAY, THIRTEENTH WEEK I Chronicles 16: 29-34.
"Fairest Lord Jesus"

Jesus is Lord—He is our "soul's glory, joy, and crown." We may sing of the beauty of meadows and woodlands in spring but this is as nothing compared to the beauty that Jesus creates in the person who comes out of sorrow into the light and joy of His peace! Jesus' light is brighter and purer than the sun or moon or stars for His light transforms and heals the darkness and bitterness of men's hearts to praise Him! All nature is created to praise for "The Lord reigns!"

Jesus, in thanksgiving for all the beauty of your creation, I praise you as Lord who has made my heart sing with joy! Amen.

FRIDAY, THIRTEENTH WEEK   Galatians 6: 14.
"In the cross of Christ I glory"

The author of this hymn, like St. Paul, has found that he can glory only in the Cross of Jesus. He gives us His peace when we surrender our lives to Him. We find in our own personal experience—when we do not bog down in self-pity—that "Bane and blessing, pain and pleasure,/By the cross are sanctified." The world has been crucified to us: it no longer has power over us. And we are crucified to the world for we no longer live in ourselves alone, but Christ Jesus dwells in us!

Thank You, Jesus, that I can personally accept Your salvation knowing You will bring me through the woes to the "glory side." Amen.

SATURDAY, THIRTEENTH WEEK I Corinthians 1: 30-31.
"Fling out the banner! let it float"

St. Paul, greatest of all missionaries, flung out the banner of the Cross of Jesus and nations have been converted as a result of his preaching Jesus Christ and Him crucified! Lost souls have been touched and unconverted nations have found spiritual rebirth. In our baptismal vows some of us promised "manfully to fight under His banner against sin, the world and the devil." Do we who sing this hymn today believe *truly* in the power of the Cross? Often we modern Christians proclaim fear, defeatism, hopelessness—no wonder there are many pagans around us! If our lives do not reflect the glory of Christ, those outside the Church will see no reason for joining with us!

Jesus, help me to fling out Your banner in praising You today. Help me to proclaim Your love, Your power, Your peace. Amen.

MONDAY, FOURTEENTH WEEK   I Peter 2: 24-25.
"How sweet the Name of Jesus sounds"

The Name of Jesus is not dear to those who have rejected Him—it is often a curse upon their lips. And some have just taken Him for granted. Have we taken Him as "Shepherd and Guardian of your souls?" Peter reminds us: "By his wounds you have been healed." Do you accept this glorious promise, or is it just a difficult passage of Scripture? If we can catch the measles from others, why not try to catch the faith of our Scripture and hymn? Is the name incurable too great for the Name of Jesus? Yes, our efforts are too often weak and our thoughts cold—like Nazareth where "he did not do many mighty works there, because of their unbelief."

Jesus, we praise You as Shepherd, Guardian, King and Lord for you are the Way and the Life. Amen.

*TUESDAY, FOURTEENTH WEEK   Romans 5: 1-8.
"Come, thou long expected Jesus"

---

* This meditation is especially suitable for the Christmas Season. If you wish to use it at that time, substitute one of the remaining devotions.

The same Lord, born as a babe in a manger, died on the Cross for our sakes and reigns eternally as King. His birth was prophesied centuries before—He was born to be King of our hearts. He came to bring release from fears and other sins. He came to bring forgiveness of sins to those who accept Him as King of Kings and Lord of Lords. When we allow Him to reign in our hearts, He establishes His Kingdom of love and peace and we find rest in Him no matter what the day may bring. As we thank Him today for being our Saviour, may we remember to pray for the unconverted, those who have not yet found His joy?

Lord, Jesus, we thank You that in great humility You came to win us, to deliver us. Let our thanks be shown in witness today to one who doesn't know Your love. Amen.

WEDNESDAY, FOURTEENTH WEEK   Psalm 100.
"All people that on earth do dwell"

Our hymn was written with Psalm 100 as its basis. If we keep this psalm in our hearts, we shall find ourselves living in a different dimension—for praise truly changes things! First, it changes our own attitudes of heart and mind as our spirits worship the Lord in songs of thanksgiving. Then our bodies begin to respond to this inner "healing climate." "Fear" means "awe" in this context for the mercy of God is awesome and "his steadfast love endures forever." No matter what happens, if we praise the Lord throughout the day, He can bring good out of evil. A friend said inwardly, "Thank You Jesus" no matter what his employer said to him—that is, he let Jesus into the place where the hurt might have come. Eventually the man was changed; and so, of course, was my friend!

Make me a channel of praise today, Lord. Amen.

THURSDAY, FOURTEENTH WEEK   St. John 3: 5.

"Blessed assurance, Jesus is mine"

How beautifully the author shares his own experiences of the Lord's blessed assurance! Resting in the Lord does not mean inactivity, but rather that our lives become a continual story, a continuing song — "Praising my Saviour all the day long." When we are "born of water and the Spirit" Jesus Christ becomes so *real* to us we can't wait to share Him with others! Our tongues are loosed in joy to praise Him who has saved us from the abyss of self-centeredness.

Blessed Saviour, I thank You for the assurance of Your precious Love which enables me to ride out the storms of life because I am "lost in Your Love," not in my own lostness. Make my healed life a song of continual praise! Amen.

FRIDAY, FOURTEENTH WEEK   Ephesians 3: 20.

"I love thy kingdom, Lord"

Is your church a beloved community where Christ can abide and those in need of His love can find refuge from the world's critical spirit and harsh ways? Does your church proclaim its wealth and numbers—or "Jesus, thou friend divine,/Our Saviour and our King"? Do words you say in church and hymns you sing translate themselves into daily faith? Can you pass on healing comfort and strength to the lonely, confused and fearful? God's truth needs to be proclaimed in the pressures of life, tested and proven to bear our weight. The Church is Christ's Body, ministering in His Name in faith and love to a broken world.

Lord, make my church not only a building but a fellowship of the concerned. In praise, help us proclaim Your love to all who enter. Amen.

SATURDAY, FOURTEENTH WEEK   Ephesians 6: 10-12.
"A mighty fortress is our God"

In this hymn by Martin Luther we see his eloquent personal convictions (which had been tested under fire) in God as "A bulwark never failing." So all that happens to us is *not* God's *intentional* Will if He is our fortress protecting us from the enemy who seeks to defeat us. While God may test our strength at times, it is *Satan who tempts us to our undoing!* But, as Luther says triumphantly, we are to be God's instruments for victory—we are not alone! We do not trust in our own power but in His.

Almighty God, we thank You for deliverance from the power of Satan through Jesus. You have won the final victory. Amen.

MONDAY, FIFTEENTH WEEK   Psalm 69: 30, 34.
"All praise to thee, my God, this night"

For those troubled with insomnia, this evening hymn of prayer might be a great blessing. It includes the five elements of true prayer: adoration, thanksgiving, penitence, intercession and petition—ending in a paean of praise. Bishop Ken's last stanza is sung as the Doxology in many different churches when the offering is presented. We need to learn to praise God in the heights and praise Him in the depths—not just when the going is easy! The Bishop praised God whether he was in favor with King Charles of England—or in disgrace!

Thanks be to God who brings good out of evil when I trust and praise Him. Amen.

*TUESDAY, FIFTEENTH WEEK   St. Matthew 2: 1-2.
"Angels, from the realms of glory"

---

* This meditation is especially suitable for the Christmas Season. If you wish to use it at that time, substitute one of the remaining devotions.

Angels, shepherds and wise men call us today to "Worship Christ, the new-born King." Our beings are so constructed that we begin to feel like what we affirm. So when we are depressed and filled with self-pity, we should begin with worship: praising God that *He* is able, even if we are not! He will protect and guide us, forgive and renew us. As we praise Him in hymn and Scripture, we turn our eyes from self to Him who will lift the burdens from our hearts and replace them with healing joy.

Jesus, we come to worship You as King of our hearts today— in spirit and in truth. Amen.

WEDNESDAY, FIFTEENTH WEEK Revelation 19: 5-7.

"Alleluia, song of gladness"

When we join with the company of angels in praising our Lord, we help to release some of His divine power into the world about us. Our eleventh century author says: "Alleluia, song of gladness/Voice of joy that cannot die." But let these words be sincere outpourings of our hearts bearing fruit in our lives, not a shameless mockery. Let us not mouth words without thinking seriously of what we are saying. We would hardly treat an earthly king thus; far less, the King of Kings!

Lord Jesus, help me today to show my praise in actions, not just words of hymn or prayer. Amen.

THURSDAY, FIFTEENTH WEEK Ephesians 1: 7.

"There is power in the Blood"

This hymn probably has little meaning to those who have never meditated on this Scripture or experienced the deliverance that the precious Blood of Jesus has made possible for them. Squeamish people do not like the thought of "power in the Blood"—but when bleeding to death they are more than happy to accept a blood transfusion! A drowning man asks no credentials of the one who saves him! Only in Christ is our release secured through the shedding of His Blood. In His forgiveness on the Cross, He has forgiven our sins. This is healing!

Jesus, I claim You now as my Saviour and I praise You for the power that Your victory on the Cross has won in my life. Amen.

FRIDAY, FIFTEENTH WEEK   I Chronicles 29: 14.
"All things are thine; no gift have we"

This hymn, often used in the service of consecration of a Church, may be sung as the Sunday offering is presented for it emphasizes praise and stewardship. It asks God to bless the building in its emptiness with His love: "And let their door a gateway be/To lead us from ourselves to thee." Many people have entered the door of a Church, out of curiosity or even to seek shelter from a storm and have found truly that the door was a "gateway" leading from self to God. Is yours?

Come, Holy Spirit, quicken and heal our sluggish hearts with gratitude for all our Father's gifts to us. Remind us that *we need* to give in thanksgiving: for the gift of ourselves is all we can lay at His feet. Amen.

SATURDAY, FIFTEENTH WEEK   Psalm 100.
"Joyful, joyful, we adore thee"

To sing a joyous hymn like this throughout the day can really drive away doubt and dissolve the petty clouds that often obscure God's blessings. The beauty of heaven and earth reflects God's Glory but His love is the greatest of all gifts to us. He is always "giving and forgiving." We are to "Serve the Lord with gladness!" and "Come into his presence with singing." Only He can lift our spirits with divine Joy. As we give praise today, we open ourselves to more of His love and joy to share with others.

Lord, I praise You because Your "steadfast love endures forever" and I am a sheep of Your pasture. Amen.

MONDAY, SIXTEENTH WEEK   Romans 12: 1-2.
"Take my life, and let it be"

God does not take our words lightly when we offer ourselves to be His workmen! To live consecrated to Jesus does not mean we must leave our jobs and go headlong into the ministry. Our Lord needs consecrated workmen in *every* area of life, providing we are doing all to His glory. There was a porter who converted an old railway car into a prayer room and carried many people to the Lord as he carried their luggage!

Jesus, I consecrate my eyes, my ears, my tongue, my hands, my mind and heart to You now. Make my life wholly Yours. Amen.

TUESDAY, SIXTEENTH WEEK   Psalm 105: 1-5.
"God of mercy, God of grace"

The psalmist emphasizes his joy in God's merciful, saving Presence. Today's hymn also stresses our need to praise God for His grace as we ask Him to "Fill Thy Church with light Divine:/And Thy saving health extend." Too often we ask for more before we thank God for all His many blessings to us. He does not need our praise as much as *we need to give it!* We are to "seek his presence continually! Remember the wonderful works that he has done, his miracles," and Rejoice!

Jesus, thank You for all my blessings; help me to live in joy. Amen.

WEDNESDAY, SIXTEENTH WEEK   Romans 5: 10-11.
"My God, I love Thee; not because"

Although St. Paul considered himself the chief sinner because of his pre-conversion persecution of Christians, he had found such joy in the forgiveness of His Lord that nothing could quench it (not even shipwreck or imprisonment). He longed to share the joy with others. Some love God because of hopes of heaven or fear of hell—but our deepest love stems not from our desire to get something but rather to love Him as He *first* loved us! Are we so ungrateful as to reject the only love that is unlimited, unchanging, unconditional?

Lord, forgive my ingratitude. Fill my heart with divine love. Amen.

THURSDAY, SIXTEENTH WEEK   I Chronicles 29: 11.

"For the beauty of the earth"

"Lord of all, to Thee we raise/This our hymn of grateful praise" is a refrain overflowing with love and joy—an antidote to the trivial complaints and self-pity that many of us harbour unwittingly in our hearts as we take for granted the love of family, the wonder of our own bodies or the beauty of earth and skies. Man's accomplishments (even walking on the moon) are nothing compared to God's marvelous creation! "*In*-gratitude is a sin against the Holy Spirit."

Lord, forgive my ingratitude that fails to exalt You because I am exalting myself or other persons. Amen.

FRIDAY, SIXTEENTH WEEK   St. Mathew 6: 28-29;
Ephesians 1: 4-5.

"All things bright and beautiful"

The miracles of God's creation refute those who would give earth's origin to haphazard causes: the tiny seed growing into a bud, the bird flying south with sure poise to avoid cold winters, are beyond man's ability to duplicate. No manmade light or heat can take the place of walking in a sunny garden after a night of cooling rain; no painted sunset quite equals the real thing! God has a divine plan for each of us: from the foundation of the world, He predestined us to be His sons and daughters.

Lord, open my eyes to see, my ears to hear, and my lips to praise the beauty of Your creation. Amen.

SATURDAY, SIXTEENTH WEEK   Ephesians 5: 18-20.
"O for a thousand tongues to sing"

Sometimes when praising the Lord, we feel there are not words to express our love! St. Paul says we are to be filled with the Holy Spirit, singing our praises to God whole-heartedly, sharing our joy (not our complaints) with one another. The Name of Jesus on our lips reminds us that our only righteousness is in Him as He, dwelling in us, brings healing to our minds and bodies through the healing of our spirits. Truly it is His "Name that charms our fears,/That bids our sorrows cease, . . ./'Tis life, and health, and peace."

Jesus, to You be all the glory for my healing. I would spread Your praise wherever I go: give me the words to witness to others. Amen.

PART 3

Hymns of Guidance

and Commitment

We need to repeat our commitment daily and often an appropriate hymn helps us to see how narrow our commitment has been. We walk by faith and not by sight—but as we take the leap of faith in committing each need or relationship to Jesus, we find that our faith grows and our spiritual eyes are opened to see and count more of His blessings. As we cry "My Lord and my God," we remember Thomas, the doubting apostle, and how often we are like him. Though we may see Jesus only dimly now, if we commit as much of ourselves as we can to as much of Him as we know, we shall daily grow in deeper understanding of His love for us—and some day we shall see Him face to face. Commitment means giving ourselves to Jesus—including our work and recreation, our private life and innermost thoughts, on dark days as well as joyous ones, at home or abroad—not just one hour on Sunday morning! We may come to this point of turning ourselves over to the Lord by a right-angled turn, a "Damascus Road experience." Or we may come over the years in a rounded curve. But whatever way, it means a turning from self to Jesus: conversion may come gradually or suddenly—but sanctification is a lifetime's work! When we commit our problems to Him we find His guidance to solve them in His higher ways. We are to commit our lives so that Jesus can direct our paths as we *trust* in Him! Then we come to know His Will and can receive wisdom and strength to fulfill it (*Romans 12: 1-2*).

Dear Lord, I give myself to You to be used however, whenever, wherever and with whomever You choose. I give You the past, the present and the future. Guide me according to Your perfect Will. Make me Your instrument of grace. Amen.

MONDAY, SEVENTEENTH WEEK   St. John 4: 13-14.
"I heard the voice of Jesus say"

Jesus told us to come to Him and rest; to "Stoop down, and drink, and live" for He gives us "living water;" to look up to Him who is "this dark world's light." Have we listened to *His* Voice today? If we hear His directions, do we really want to follow His Way? Will we dare to abandon our self-will to stake our life on Him who is The Life? To walk in His light is better than to follow any known path.

Jesus, lead me in Your way all through this day. Amen.

TUESDAY, SEVENTEENTH WEEK   Ephesians 6: 11.
"Stand up, stand up, for Jesus!"

How often we sing this without taking the words to heart! We go on in life trusting in our human strength when we should "Put on the Gospel armor," each piece put on with prayer. How little time we spend praying for the pulling down of the strongholds of Satan in the hearts of those who are breaking homes or leading young people astray! We are so preoccupied with our own aches that we fail Christ in the strife of evil about us. He needs "prayer warriors."

Lord, make me preoccupied with the needs of others, not my own; make me a "soldier of the Cross." Amen.

WEDNESDAY, SEVENTEENTH WEEK   Psalm 36: 7-10.
"Guide me, O thou great Jehovah"

Doctors often remind us that prolonged negative emotions tend to cause functional disease. Each of us is a "Pilgrim through this barren land." To pray "Guide me, O thou great Jehovah" can save us from building up inner tensions. We shall worry less if we hold the thought: "In thy light do we see light." When ill we can sing: "Open now the crystal fountains/Whence the living waters flow"—and visualize ourselves being healed rather than anticipating worse pain!

Daily Devotions::43

Lord, keep me "upright of heart," not downcast with fear. Amen.

THURSDAY, SEVENTEENTH WEEK St. John 1: 1-5.
"Lead, kindly Light"

When gloom and despair press in upon us, we must turn to the Light of Christ to lead us out and onward. It helps to hold to the words of our hymn "Lead thou me on . . . I do not ask to see/The distant scene; one step enough for me." His Life is our Light—"The light shines in the darkness, and the darkness has not overcome it." Often our answer will not come as quickly as putting a coin in a vending machine! But it will be there when needed.

Lord, make me a patient follower whom You can lead, one step at a time. Amen.

FRIDAY, SEVENTEENTH WEEK Psalm 25: 4-10.
"Lead us, heavenly Father, lead us"

This thought in the first stanza moves on to "Saviour, breathe forgiveness o'er us;/All our weakness thou dost know." Our God is not "way out there," but has dwelt among us and knows our earthly woes! We are reminded that God is our Father, our Saviour and the Holy Spirit who descends to "Fill out hearts with heavenly joy." Our hymn ends gloriously: "Thus provided, pardoned, guided,/Nothing can our peace destroy."

Father, keep me always joyously aware of Your guiding, forgiving, empowering Love. Amen.

SATURDAY, SEVENTEENTH WEEK St. Luke 11: 2-4.
"Thy Kingdom come, O God"

We say the Lord's Prayer so often that it almost becomes a mechanical response to the words "Our Father." When we pray thus, are we willing to be a part of God's answer? Are we rallying to His cause as our hymn says: "Thy rule, O Christ, begin"—in our hearts so that we may be used by Him to "break with thine iron rod/The tyrannies of sin"? Are we seeking healing just to get well, or so that we may be a part of His redemptive work in bringing in His "reign of peace?"

Jesus, use me today to manifest Your Love. Amen.

MONDAY, EIGHTEENTH WEEK St. Matthew 28: 19-20.
"Lord, speak to me, that I may speak"

Too often, alas, we speak without praying the words of today's hymn. We condemn, instead of seeking to lead errants to Him who alone is Judge—who came not to judge but to save! We need to consecrate our lives to Him that He can teach us, lead us, fill us and use us in *His* ministry of healing, forgiving love to those in need. We are to see people and situations as Jesus sees them; to listen only to things that He would hear; to think and speak only as He would do.

Jesus, make me a channel of Your Grace to others today. Amen.

TUESDAY, EIGHTEENTH WEEK Ephesians 3: 14-19.
"My God, accept my heart this day"

At confirmation we have prayed (or been prayed for) in a prayer similar to St. Paul's. We have sung today's hymn with ardor—but this is not a once-in-a-lifetime matter. It should be a *daily* prayer: "My God, accept my heart this day,/And make it always thine,/That I from thee no more may stray." Even though we stray daily we must not lose faith and heart! We are not made into Christ's image overnight, but we are *becoming* "rooted and grounded in love"—*His* Love!

Lord, dwell in my heart through faith, that I may be filled with Your fullness. Amen.

WEDNESDAY, EIGHTEENTH WEEK   I Corinthians 13: 12.

"God moves in a mysterious way"

Life is often to us like puzzling images seen in a mirror, because our knowledge is only partial. We sing: "Judge not the Lord by feeble sense,/But trust him for his grace;/Behind a frowning providence/He hides a smiling face." Yet how often when He says "No" to our prayers, we become petulant like spoiled children and turn away from the very Source of grace we need most! "God is his own interpreter,/And he will make it plain" echoes "then I shall understand fully, even as I have been fully understood."

Lord, have Your own way and help me to want it! Amen.

THURSDAY, EIGHTEENTH WEEK   I John 4: 9-11.

"New every morning is the love"

We need awareness of "New mercies . . . /New perils past, new sins forgiven,/New thoughts of God, new hopes of heaven," as the hymn says. As we let in God's Love, we can see more of heaven all about us, transforming old experiences. "help us, this and every day,/To live more nearly as we pray." Fine words must be practised, not just sung or prayed. Prayers must be lived out in the "laboratory of life" if we are to be brought nearer to God daily.

God of Love, fill our petty minds and our critical hearts with an overflow of Your love. Amen.

FRIDAY, EIGHTEENTH WEEK   Genesis 2: 7; 15-17.

"Breathe on me, Breath of God"

The problem of wanting God's Will is always with us on this side of the grave. We are not even able to surrender our own wills without His help. The riddle of world problems would be solved if only people could love as God loves and do as He does—*every* person! Original sin is our choosing our own way, not *His.* Homes are broken by divorce, children are emotionally retarded, wives or husbands break down mentally—because one is unable to love the other.

Father, breathe Your Holy Spirit into me so I can truly love and live as You would have me. Amen.

SATURDAY, EIGHTEENTH WEEK   St. Mark 16: 15-16.
"From Greenland's icy mountains"

As we sing these words, does it make any appreciable impact on our missionary giving? "Salvation, O salvation!/The joyful sound proclaim,/Till each remotest nation/Has learn't Messiah's name." Do we *really* care whether Christ is worshiped in Greenland or Africa—enough to give up some stained glass window? Have we denied "the lamp of life," the Redeemer, to those who have not heard His good news because our too little is *too late?* Are we willing to give a son or daughter to be our Lord's messenger?

Jesus, forgive me for my lack of concern about carrying Your Name to others. Amen.

MONDAY, NINETEENTH WEEK   St. John 14: 16-17.
"Come, gracious Spirit, heavenly Dove"

God in His mercy draws us to Him through the working of the Holy Spirit whom Jesus promised to send to lead us into all Truth: "The light of truth to us display,/And make us know and choose thy way." How often we bring illness upon ourselves because we do not choose *His* Way of Love; or because we worry instead of trusting our needs and our loved ones to Him! The Holy Spirit is God in action in the world and we can live by His Power and Wisdom when we receive Him to dwell in our hearts.

Holy Spirit, bring forth in my life Your fruit of peace, love, joy, patience, humility. Amen.

TUESDAY, NINETEENTH WEEK St. John 10: 2-5.

"Saviour, like a shepherd lead us"

Jesus is the Good Shepherd who calls us, His sheep, by name and leads us into green pastures. Like sheep, we learn to recognize the Shepherd's Voice by continuous listening for His call. He cares equally for each sheep: "he goes before them, and the sheep follow him, for they know his voice. A stranger they will not follow." Too often we humans do follow the strange voices tempting us into pastures that are out of bounds: cults, spiritualism, reincarnation. If only we would learn to discern Jesus' Voice from the siren voices! Jesus bought us at a price and He loves us even when we stray. He will lead us back into the fold when we pray.

Blessed Jesus, lead me today like a shepherd for I belong to You. Amen.

WEDNESDAY, NINETEENTH WEEK Psalm 63: 1-5.

"O for a closer walk with God"

The psalmist tells us of his own experience of walking with God: that His "steadfast love is better than life"—far better! Yes, God is truly *our* God! He "created us for Himself and our hearts are restless until we find rest in Him", wrote St. Augustine. We need to identify in our lives the idols that *usurp God's place* so that we can take them off the throne. Our sins separate us from God; and many of us cry out in despair the opening words of this hymn, especially when we realize we have failed Him. God in His merciful Love is ever ready to forgive and restore us to His Peace—*when we repent.*

Father, keep me in a closer walk with You as I re-commit my day to You. Amen.

THURSDAY, NINETEENTH WEEK St. John 20: 26-29.

"O Jesus, I have promised"

How glibly we promise to serve Jesus faithfully to the end—
yet too often we fail Him! Like the disciples, we become
weary; our wills become clouded by selfishness or fear of
failure; we are blinded. This hymn of commitment acknowl-
edges our human frailty, our need to hear Jesus' Voice "In
accents clear and still", to feel His Presence as Friend and to
receive His Grace as Master. We are to serve Him by following
Him, not our own ideas of service. When we do, we experience His Peace as our Guardian and Guide.

Jesus, be to me eternally my Master and Friend, my Guardian
and Guide. Give me Grace (Wisdom and Strength) to serve
You today. Amen.

FRIDAY, NINETEENTH WEEK   Revelation 3: 20.
"O Jesus, thou art standing"

Some of us have wept in penitence while singing this hymn
which reminds us of the way we have kept the door of our
hearts barred while Jesus waited patiently for many years. In
Holman Hunt's magnificent picture, Jesus is shown standing
at the door knocking but there is no lock on the outside: we
alone can open our hearts. He will not force His way because
He has given us freedom of will to accept or reject Him. His
hand and brow bear marks of wounds and thorns as He
reminds us gently that He died for *us*. Will we leave Him
standing or cry: "Dear Saviour, enter, enter,/And leave us
nevermore"?

Come into my heart now, dear Saviour, to stay forever.
Amen.

SATURDAY, NINETEENTH WEEK   Philippians 3: 10-12.
"Awake, my soul, stretch every nerve"

In the "heavenly race" of life, we are to go forward. God
calls us to the precious goal of eternal life which begins *now*
as we know Christ, "becoming like him in his death." St. Paul

reminds us that the race will not be easy for we may have to share Christ's sufferings—being misunderstood or rejected for His sake. This apostle does not claim "to have arrived spiritually." Dr. E. Stanley Jones said, "We are Christians in the making." You and I may not be famous missionaries but we can respond to God's call with renewed vigor, committing mind, soul and body—because, as our Scripture says, "Christ Jesus has made me his own."

Lord, keep me faithful in the testings of life and make me all Your own. Amen.

MONDAY, TWENTIETH WEEK   St. Matthew 28: 19-20.
"Christ for the world we sing"

Like thousands of other missionaries we are to help bring the world to Christ. This hymn describes the poor, the sorrowful, and weak: "Sin-sick and sorrow-worn,/Whom Christ doth heal." It is Christ who redeems the wayward and lost. Today in our Churches there are many whose attractive exteriors cover broken hearts! Psychiatrists' offices are filled with patients, many of whom could find victory over their despair if only they could turn themselves over to Christ. Will you help?

Lord Jesus, let my love for You today rub off on one of my neighbors. Let my faith be catching in the dry wood of an unbeliever's heart. Amen.

TUESDAY, TWENTIETH WEEK   St. Luke 10: 2.
"Come, labor on"

The Lord calls us to be laborers in His vineyard for the harvest potential is great but few are willing to seek His Will for their lives. Many parents encourage their children to choose careers leading to wealth, intellect or power—and how few pray for them to follow the Lord's purposes! Our hymn reminds us that God fulfills His plans through weak, ordinary persons. We have no time to rest on past laurels. Regardless of age or station, in life *each* of us can bear the Good News. Are you willing?

Master, show me Your Will for my life and give me Your courage, wisdom and strength to fulfill it. Amen.

WEDNESDAY, TWENTIETH WEEK I Corinthians 3: 11-14.
"Go, labor on! spend and be spent!"

We are building on the foundation, Jesus Christ, as we commit ourselves to "spend and be spent" in helping to bring in God's Kingdom. His fire will test our labors and none will be in vain if we work to His glory, not our own! We may feel faint or lazy at times, but if the work is to survive we must continue in vigilant prayer for the soul that needs to be won to Christ. The "world's highway" is our missionary field where we shall find those needing to build their lives on the Rock of Jesus. Our reward will come from *Him* as we find joy in being *His laborers*.

Lord, make me willing to give of myself unstintingly to draw others closer to You. Amen.

THURSDAY, TWENTIETH WEEK   Ephesians 2: 10.
"I sought the Lord, and afterward I knew"

The wonder of God's Love is that *He* is always seeking us—more than we are Him! After we find Him, we can look back and see how often He answered our needs before we prayed. How often He has been silently with us to keep us from sinking in the storms of life. He takes hold of the situations we give Him—for He has loved us from the foundation of the world. We are found by Him in our lostness in life—and by His Grace we are healed as we commit ourselves to the purposes which He has already prepared for us.

Saviour, lead me, protect me, fill me, use me in Your work of Love. Amen.

FRIDAY, TWENTIETH WEEK   Ephesians 4: 15-16.
"Jesus, with thy Church abide"

We are the Church, the Body of which Christ is the Head. This litany calls us as members to pray for the Church to become the instrument our Lord can use to "Overthrow the hosts of sin" so that the lost and brokenhearted, the poor and blind can be ministered to in His Name. Once a man attended the first service of a healing conference and found the spirit of love and prayer so compelling that he returned for every subsequent meeting instead of going to the ball games as he had planned! Is your church such a committed one that a stranger would feel compelled to return?

Jesus, revive and renew Your Church—beginning with me! Amen.

SATURDAY, TWENTIETH WEEK   Ephesians 6: 11-13.
"Onward, Christian soldiers"

How glibly we sing this hymn without making it a serious commitment! St. Paul warns us of the reality of "spiritual hosts of wickedness in the heavenly places." Too many today are casualties in the battle being waged by powers of evil against His Body the Church. Too many others complacently sing, "Like a mighty army/Moves the Church of God" and do nothing the rest of the week to claim Christ's victory over Satan in the lives about us! When a "prayer warrior" is struck down by the enemy (Satan) do we carry him from the battlefield on stretchers of loving, healing prayers? Or do we condemn him and lose faith?

Lord, make me truly Your "prayer warrior" as I now commit my life to Your army of compassion. Amen.

MONDAY, TWENTY-FIRST WEEK   Exodus 13: 21-22
and St. John 14:6.
"Lamp of our feet, whereby we trace"

52::Hymns of Guidance and Commitment

In a pillar of cloud by day and of fire by night, God led the Israelites from Egypt through the wilderness. How often when praying for guidance we wish for such a clear sign! Our hymn reminds us that the Word of God can impart His wisdom and be a "Lamp of our feet" to enable us to find His pathways when we are straying or befuddled. Jesus is the bread of the world, the manna we need today in our hearts. If we are teachable—*childlike*, not childish—He will lead us: for He *is* "the way, and the truth, and the life."

Jesus, roll away the fog of self-will as I commit my life to You for healing and guidance. Amen.

TUESDAY, TWENTY-FIRST WEEK   I Peter 2: 6-10.
"O Sion, haste, thy mission high fulfilling"

Our mission as those who believe in God and have experienced His mercy is to tell the Good News to the world. *He* is the Light, the love they are hungering for in our confused times! There is no generation gap among Christians of all ages who love the Lord. *We* are the "chosen race"—redeemed by Jesus, the new Adam. *We* are a "royal priesthood"—the priesthood of all believers. *We* are needed to "declare the wonderful deeds of him who called you out of darkness into his marvelous light." Do we dare ask God for more healing when we have not yet witnessed to what He has given?

God, I commit myself to be Your witness today. Heal me of my shyness and share Your love through me. Amen.

WEDNESDAY, TWENTY-FIRST WEEK   Isaiah 1: 15-20.
"Rise up, O men of God"

Too often we are preoccupied with petty injustices of the past in our own lives when we should be far more concerned with ending past wrongs our civilization has inflicted upon others of other races. We need to dispense with lesser things and concentrate our attention as our Scripture tells us: to "seek justice, correct oppression; defend the fatherless, plead for the widow." Ours is not a faith of incense within stained glass windows. The Church is unequal to its redemptive mission unless *we all* lift the Cross of Jesus in our daily relationships. How can we presume to pray for our own healing if we are callous to the needs of others?

O God, help me to rise up and serve You as my King. Amen.

THURSDAY, TWENTY-FIRST WEEK   Joshua 24: 15.
"Once to every man and nation"

Originally, this hymn was a poem of protest against military action toward another nation. There are times when we must be brave and make a choice that comes only once to a nation as to whether our witness will be on the side of good or of evil. Although the cause of the latter may seem for awhile to prosper, we can trust God to watch over His own. The true meaning of "bearing thy Cross" is taking a stand against injustice, no matter what the personal cost may be. This may be necessary today for the healing of races and nations.

Lord, make us as a nation an instrument of Your justice and bring us Your healing Peace. Amen.

FRIDAY, TWENTY-FIRST WEEK   St. John 8: 12.
"Let the lower lights be burning"

Are we keepers of our Father's "lighthouse?" How many have wholeheartedly accepted this job of radiating the Light of Christ? Have we spoken a word of praise and encouragement in Christ's Name to some shipwrecked sailor, one obviously despondent? Or provided an alternative for one tempted—remembering that, but for God's Grace, we might stand in his shoes? God judges our self-righteousness, our scathing judgments—more harshly than the sins we condemn in others! We qualify as "lower lights" and we have a job to do: "Send a gleam across the wave!/Some poor fainting, struggling seaman,/You may rescue, you may save!" *Try* it!

Father, thank You for sending Your Light to me in Jesus. Help me today to be a light-bearer to someone in darkness. Amen.

SATURDAY, TWENTY-FIRST WEEK   Acts 7: 51-60.
"The Son of God goes forth to war"

As we sing this hymn and read the story of Stephen's martyrdom, do we ever wonder if our own faith could stand the acid test? Too often we are like James and John who wanted the honor of sitting at Jesus' right hand, but are we *really* able to drink from His cup? Is our commitment deep enough, our faith firm enough, to be tested in the fire of persecution like the saints of old? *This* is Christian suffering—not the aches and pains of illness, but the willingness to stand up and be counted for Christ, even though the cost is life itself!

Lord, give us Your Grace to bear the Cross of persecution, to follow in Your footsteps and pray for those who persecute us. Amen.

MONDAY, TWENTY-SECOND WEEK   Psalm 37: 5-8.
"He leadeth me! O blessed thought"

How often we Christians want to be guided but without paying the price of real commitment! We want to be led but only beside still waters: we too often turn back or revile God when the going is rough. "I prayed but nothing happened" we complain too often. Are we "Content, whatever lot I see,/Since 'tis my God that leadeth me"? Our hymn reminds us that there will be "scenes of deepest gloom" as well as "By waters calm." If we are willing to commit our ways to the Lord, trusting in Him, we need not fear.

God, I commit myself to You; guide me now. Amen.

TUESDAY, TWENTY-SECOND WEEK   St. Mark 4: 36-41.

"Jesus, Saviour, pilot me"

Many of us love the picture of Jesus as Helmsman standing behind the boy to pilot him over the stormy seas of life. We remember how the Lord said "Be still!" and even the wind and waves obeyed. As we contemplate treacherous rocks and unknown shores ahead in the voyage of life, He says to us, "Have you no faith?" A passenger in a storm-tossed plane, felt led in the Name of Jesus to command the winds to subside and in a moment there was an almost unbelievable peace. Some of us prayed in this faith during a sudden storm on the Sea of Galilee and it became calm.

Saviour, pilot me today through calm or storm in perfect peace of mind and spirit. Amen.

WEDNESDAY, TWENTY-SECOND WEEK
St. Matthew 25: 31-46.

"O Master, let me walk with thee"

In this passage of Scripture we are told that what we do to the humblest child of God, we have done to Jesus—a thought we need to face daily. Have we welcomed the stranger, fed the hungry and visited those sick or in prison? Have we walked with the Master in paths of service to others less fortunate? Have we tried to win someone to Jesus by showing His love? Or guided the wayward to Him? We need to pray for His patience, His triumphant trust, His peace so that we can show His healing Love to others, not just our weak intermittent human love that too often depends on *their* "good behavior."

Master, help me to show Your healing love to those in need about me today. Amen.

THURSDAY, TWENTY-SECOND WEEK
St. Luke 22: 41-46.

"Have Thine own way, Lord"

How hard it is to say "Have Thine own way, Lord"—and *really mean it!* Self-will keeps cropping up in situations even when we have committed our lives and sincerely seek to live according to His Will. The more attuned we are to God's Voice, the more we hear His still, small promptings. The more we obey, the more guidance we shall receive: the more aware we shall become that His Way really is the *best* way! Often, like Christ at Gethsemane, we pray that the Cross in our lives may be removed, but many times it is only by *going through* the Cross (as He did) that we can find the *highest* victory!

Lord, help me to will Your Will! Even when I don't want to accept some difficult pathway, help me to know it will lead me closer to You. Amen.

FRIDAY, TWENTY-SECOND WEEK   St. John 6: 35-40.

"Just as I am, without one plea"

How wonderful to know that Christ accepts us, just as we are! This is hard for us to believe because often our friends and family don't. Too often we think that we must be all cleaned up to come to Jesus. Too often we bring Him our talents but not our sins—yet He is the only one who can cleanse and redeem us by His forgiving love. His Blood was shed for me: "poor, wretched, blind;/Sight, riches, healing of the mind;/Yea all I need, in Thee to find." Do I really want Him?

"O Lamb of God, I come." Amen.

SATURDAY, TWENTY-SECOND WEEK
St. Matthew 4: 18-22.

"Jesus calls us; o'er the tumult"

Jesus calls us through our own particular tumult; a broken heart when one we love has failed us; the earthly loss of one who, via death, has stepped into eternal life; deliverance in some dreadful accident or illness; the vision of Him as seen in one of His disciples, ancient or modern; a flash of revelation when life makes sense only if it is given to Him; the "still small Voice"; illumined Scripture we never noticed before!

Jesus, help me to recognize Your Voice in the din of everyday life. Help me to obey your call—first! Amen.

MONDAY, TWENTY-THIRD WEEK   I John 5: 20.
"God be in my head"

We cannot say one thing and do the opposite without confusing that marvelous deep mind which records all. Our consciences prick us and make us disturbed. We can continue to push this down until some day a crisis breaks through the inner wall and the accumulation of repressed guilt erupts in a depression that seems to engulf us. How much better to pray for God to be in our understanding, looking, speaking, and thinking throughout the day; and at its end, to ask His forgiveness and help to do better the next day: to right the failures by His Grace!

God, be in all of me all the time. Amen.

TUESDAY, TWENTY-THIRD WEEK   St. John 14: 21-24.
"Day by day"

This thirteenth century prayer of St. Richard of Chichester reminds us that commitment is not a one-time experience but a continuous, day-by-day process of learning to know and love and obey our Lord. The world may not recognize Jesus: but we "see Him" as we follow His commandments. He has promised to come and make His home in the hearts of those who love Him, those who in obedience keep His words and do His Will. Are *you* being obedient to all that He has shown you of His Will for your life?

Lord, make me willing today to see areas where I have not been obedient; forgive me and fill me with Your healing Love. Amen.

WEDNESDAY, TWENTY-THIRD WEEK
Philippians 4: 8-9.
"Father, we thank thee for the night"

This favorite hymn for children makes adults more aware of the blessings of God's creation. We need to thank Him—and not take for granted—our rest and food and morning light. We need to express our gratitude by showing love to others— yet how much of the time God's gifts of sight and speech are *misused*; to see and dwell on things that are spiritually harmful to us; and to gossip, which brings harm to others! How often we forget that we were created "to glorify God and enjoy Him forever"; and to love, forgive and understand our fellow men as He loves, forgives and accepts us!

Almighty Creator, forgive me for accepting Your wonders with ingratitude or indifference. Help me to see and tell the good news of Your healing, loving care. Amen.

THURSDAY, TWENTY-THIRD WEEK   Philippians 2: 9-11.
"At the Name of Jesus Every knee shall bow"

We sing bravely "Crown Him as your Captain/In temptation's hour." Jesus of Nazareth ransomed sinful humanity from the fall whether or not the world believes it. As God incarnate, He saves us by His Grace from the prison of our own self-centeredness, our self-worship, self-pity, self-dependence, self-consciousness, self-hate. His love converts us: turns us around so that our lives can reflect His radiant glory instead of our own shabbiness. His Love—unconditional, unlimited—

takes us off our own pedestals (or those others have put us upon) so that we can truly praise and worship *Him* for in His Love we can bear to see ourselves as we really are! We can truly commit our lives to Him who now saves us from self-destruction.

Jesus, be Lord in my heart, in the midst of racial strife, in broken homes, in the hearts of delinquent young people. Bring healing to all of Your children to unite us as we praise and acknowledge You our Saviour today. Amen.

FRIDAY, TWENTY-THIRD WEEK   Revelation 3: 20.
"Softly and tenderly Jesus is calling"

This hymn begins where we need to begin: opening our closed hearts to Jesus who is "softly and tenderly . . ./Calling for you and for me . . ./Patiently . . . waiting and watching." How often people complain "God doesn't hear my prayers" —but they have never really *opened* their hearts to Him! Jesus stands at the door but His knock is very gentle: He does not force His way or invade our God-given freedom of will! Sometimes He knocks when illness strikes us or disaster threatens us or death seems to engulf us in grief. He is waiting to hear us say daily: "Come, Lord, abide in my heart—not as transient guest but as King. I've come home to You at last."

Jesus, come into my heart now and make it Your permanent home. Clean out all the rubbish—sinful thoughts, petty grudges, selfish habits. Make my life usable from now on—to Your Glory! Amen.

SATURDAY, TWENTY-THIRD WEEK   Romans 6: 6.
"And can it be that I should gain"

Those who call this "gospel hymn" outdated may never have experienced the depths of sin that a certain prisoner lived in for many years—yet "but for the grace of God" they might have stood in his prison cell! Both his parents died broken-hearted having tried to save their son from the penalty of his sin: yet finally the "amazing Love" of Jesus overwhelmed and lifted him in his prison cell and made him into a new person! Starr Dailey has been a channel of Jesus' love to delinquents and many have turned from the way of crime to *The Way* of Jesus because of his radiant, compelling witness. His purpose in life was to praise His Saviour. What is yours?

Loving Father, thank You for accepting us prodigals when we turn from our sins and return to You. Show us how to witness to others (as part of our commitment to You) in Your love so that they will be drawn closer to You. Amen.

PART 4

Hymns of Comfort

and Strength

God's mercies endure forever and we find this to be particularly true as each day we link our Bible reading with a hymn of comfort and strength. When we are downcast, we tend to attract more trouble to ourselves. Even Job said that the thing he had feared had come upon him. If we turn our eyes and hearts from fears and sorrows by an act of will as we sing the "hymn of the day," to our surprise, we shall find peace. Instead of concentrating on the negatives, our thoughts will be turned to Jesus, the Author and Finisher of our faith! His Love will be fanned to a flame in our hearts as we sing of His care for us. We shall begin to *feel like what we sing!* This is not being hypocritical: it is standing on the promises of God—acting in faith to let Him use the Scripture and hymns to lift our spirits with words of comfort and strength.

Father of all mercies, I thank You for Your Love and for the gifts of comfort and strength to meet each day's testings. Make the forgiveness of Jesus so real to me that I may receive and give to others His peace. Make Your Holy Spirit such an abiding Presence in my heart that I may have wisdom and strength: to be and to do Your will. Amen.

MONDAY, TWENTY-FOURTH WEEK   St. Matthew 11: 28.
"Art thou weary, art thou laden"

How many times have we come to Jesus "weary, laden, distressed" with burdens too big for us to bear and problems too difficult for us to solve! Our Lord waits with outstretched arms saying, "Come to me . . . and I will give you rest." If we find Him, follow and stay close to Him, will He bless us and vanquish our sorrow at last? "Yes!" reply not only saints and martyrs but all who have surrendered themselves to Him—believing.

As I relinquish my burdens to You, Lord, I thank You that Your peace possesses me. Help me to leave them in Your hands. Amen.

TUESDAY, TWENTY-FOURTH WEEK   St. John 6: 48-51.
"Bread of the world, in mercy broken"

Jesus is the "living bread" whom we receive at Holy Communion under the forms of the bread and wine. Because He broke the power of sin, we can be delivered if we accept His sacrifice for us personally. As we feed on Him in our hearts with thanksgiving at the Eucharist, we receive assurance ". . . That by thy grace our souls are fed" unto life eternal. As we pray for healing, let us feed on "the bread of life."

Lord Jesus, look on my sorrowing, sinful heart as now in spirit I receive Your living Bread for eternity. Amen.

WEDNESDAY, TWENTY-FOURTH WEEK   Ephesians 2: 8.
"Beneath the cross of Jesus"

Healing cults overlook the Cross but "the healing mercies of the Lord Jesus Christ" whom we proclaim are centered in the Atonement. As I look upon the Cross of Jesus, I sing of "The wonders of redeeming love,/And my own worthlessness." St. Paul wrote: "by grace you have been saved through faith; and this is not your own doing, it is the gift of God." The Power of Jesus saves us from the power of sin (often working in us to create disease) if we trust in Him, not ourselves.

Father, let the glory of the Cross be more real than my sufferings. Let me not bog down in self-pity but keep my eyes on Jesus. Amen.

THURSDAY, TWENTY-FOURTH WEEK
Ephesians 6: 10-18.
"Christian, dost thou see them"

Christian suffering is that undertaken voluntarily as part of Christ's warfare against the powers of evil that are rampant in the world about us. St. Paul warns: "Put on the whole armor of God, that you may be able to stand against the wiles of the devil. For we are not contending against flesh and blood, but against . . . the powers, against the world rulers of this present darkness . . . Pray at all times in the Spirit." We may help to bear Christ's Cross but our joy is in Him: ". . . that toil shall make thee/Some day all mine own,/And the end of sorrow/Shall be near my throne."

Lord, what I sing, help me to live today and always. Amen.

FRIDAY, TWENTY-FOURTH WEEK   Philippians 3: 13-14.
"Fight the good fight with all thy might"

We sing "Christ is the path, and Christ the prize" and then proceed to follow our own paths to our own selfish goals. How often our illness stems from this. We need to repent. "Cast care aside, lean on thy Guide, . . . Trust . . . Faint not nor fear, . . . Only believe"—easier sung than done! Yet doctors tell us that heart disease, ulcers, etc., are often caused by worry, fear, tension. As we pray for healing so that we may glorify Jesus, let it be with thanksgiving, not fear!

Jesus, be all in all to me today and always. Amen.

SATURDAY, TWENTY-FOURTH WEEK

II Corinthians 12: 9.

"Lord Jesus, think on me"

St. Paul's thorn in the flesh has often been misunderstood. Our Lord not only forgives sins but He sets us free from the power of sin! When we claim His purity and love, His grace is sufficient for our every need. We are weak—we shall always be so—but in our weakness His strength is perfected if we allow Him—not our resentments, pride, fears or self-pity—to possess us! He casts out the demons of pride, fear, jealousy, hatred, but we must give ourselves wholly to Him!

Jesus, be Lord of my emotions and my will. Amen.

MONDAY, TWENTY-FIFTH WEEK

Ephesians 4: 4-6.

"Blest be the tie that binds"

Some of us have sung this hymn, tearfully yet joyfully, in a foreign land, as we parted from Christian friends we knew we would probably not see again in this life. These words brought comfort, a blessed awareness that "The fellowship of Christian minds/Is like to that above." As St. Paul proclaims, there was no separation: neither race nor nationality, color nor creed! We were one in Christ and His love broke down barriers and prejudices. Together we had held communion with Him; we had shared burdens in His healing Presence.

Lord, make us all one. Amen.

TUESDAY, TWENTY-FIFTH WEEK

Isaiah 53: 10-12.

"The strife is o'er, the battle done"

At my mother's funeral this hymn was a keynote to the "joyous graduation" of a lifelong Christian from the bonds of senility into the "Larger Life." "Lord, by the stripes which wounded Thee,/From death's dread sting Thy servants free." There is no more fear of death for the Christian: if we live with Christ in this life, we shall live with Him in an even nearer and dearer relationship in the life to come! Because He rose from the dead, so shall we also rise to dwell with Him for all eternity.

Lord Jesus, help me to show forth Your victory in my life today. Set me free of all fear of death. Amen.

WEDNESDAY, TWENTY-FIFTH WEEK   Psalm 57: 1-3.
"Jesus, Lover of my soul"

Jesus saves us for living—as well as for dying! He is our refuge no matter what the storm. We can count on Him to comfort and support us when others fail us, when circumstances overwhelm us, when grief engulfs or loneliness shrouds us in deep depression. He will guide us safely through the pitfalls of life; and no abyss is too deep for Him, for He is merciful, He is the "Lover of my soul." He woos me and draws me to Himself, forgiving me, no matter how often I reject Him.

"Let the healing streams abound;/Make and keep me pure within," Lord. Amen.

THURSDAY, TWENTY-FIFTH WEEK St. Matthew 8: 16-17.
"At even, when the sun was set"

Although we may not see Jesus as those who are sick come to His altar, we can "know and feel that thou art here." He comes to the sad, the physically and mentally ill, those who have ignored Him out of ignorance or willfulness. His searching eyes penetrate our hearts to show us the very "skeletons in the closet" we have tried hardest to hide!

Lord Jesus, who healed the sick in Your earthly ministry, show me if some secret fear or resentment is causing my illness, poisoning my body as it poisons my mind and soul. Touch me, heal me with Your ancient power. Amen.

FRIDAY, TWENTY-FIFTH WEEK   St. John 15:5.
"Abide with me"

This hymn reminds us not only of Christ's salvation for dying, but also for living! "When other helpers fail and comforts flee,/Help of the helpless, O abide with me." If we fail to turn to Christ, we become stoics determined to beat life; or, embittered in heart, we are apt, in time, to produce brokenness or disease in our bodies and minds. St. John exhorts us to abide in Christ and let Him bear fruit through our lives as we make Him our "guide and stay . . . through cloud and sunshine." He takes away our fears of foes, illness, even death!

"In life, in death, O Lord, abide with me." Amen.

SATURDAY, TWENTY-FIFTH WEEK   Romans 8: 38-39.
"Nearer, my God, to thee"

Our hymn ends in joyous anticipation of the "Larger Life", "Nearer, my God, to thee." Troubles may seem to overwhelm us, death may threaten us, but in faith we sing: "Nearer to thee!/E'en though it be a cross/That raiseth me." There must be a cross in our hearts when we give ourselves to our Lord and let the crossbeam of His love turn the old upright of self-centeredness into a plus: a new and more wonderful sense of values! Nothing can then separate us from Him for He uses each testing to draw us to Him.

Lord God of heaven and earth, prepare me here for Your eternal Life. Amen.

MONDAY, TWENTY-SIXTH WEEK   St. Luke 7: 22-23.
"Thou to Whom the sick and dying"

We are reminded in this hymn: "May each child of Thine be willing,/Willing both in hand and heart,/All the law of love fulfilling." Are we always willing to give up some long-held grudge and fulfill the law of love? Arthritis is often relieved and healed when love replaces hate. Psychosomatic medicine attributes emotional causes to types of asthma, skin eruptions, and ulcers. Can we honestly ask God for His touch of healing and not let Him touch and heal the cause?

Lord, help me to will Your Will; give Your forgiving spirit to this person. Amen.

TUESDAY, TWENTY-SIXTH WEEK   Ephesians 5: 23-33.
"The Church's one foundation"

St. Paul, in describing Christ's relationship to the Church, compares it with holy matrimony. The Bride is not perfect: she is still torn today by schisms and distressed by heresies as our hymn reminds us. But the Bridegroom loves the Bride whom He bought at a price: He died that the Church might live. *We* are the Church. We may come from many nations but we share one Lord, one foundation, one help in Him, one goal—"because we are members of his body." It is a mystery —like holy marriage, a divine union. When marriage takes on this quality of love, husband and wife are truly blessed! Their home becomes a "little church."

Lord, make me a more effective member of Your Body, the Church, more aware of the needs of my fellow members. Amen.

WEDNESDAY, TWENTY-SIXTH WEEK   Psalm 23.
"The King of love my shepherd is"

Our shepherd is the King of Love who leads us beside still waters and restores our souls. He leads us through life and "through the valley of the shadow of death." We need have no fear of evil for His Presence comforts and protects us. At times our joy overflows when He fills our cup. He anoints our heads with healing oil. A good prescription for those who are worried is to repeat this psalm and sing this hymn throughout the day—until the tensions are dissolved in the subconscious mind and joy (in gratitude to the Lord) is released.

Lord, Your love never fails me. Help me not to fail to praise You. Amen.

THURSDAY, TWENTY-SIXTH WEEK
I Corinthians 11: 26-32.

"O God, unseen yet ever near"

We feel God's unseen Presence as we kneel at His altar in holy awe to receive the sacrament of Holy Communion. In obedience, we thus "proclaim the Lord's death until he comes." As St. Paul warns in this Scripture, we are to examine ourselves so that we will *not* unworthily eat the bread or drink of the cup which symbolize both the Old Testament manna and the New Covenant Body of the Lord; the Old Testament desert streams and the New Covenant Blood shed for us. A maid once displeased her employer because, although she did many chores well, she failed to do the appointed ones. Are we weak and sick today because of disobedience? Have we not discerned the Lord's Body?

Jesus, show me where I've been disobedient. Keep me in the stream of Your Will. Feed me with Your "heavenly food." Amen.

FRIDAY, TWENTY-SIXTH WEEK
St. Luke 2: 13-14.

"O God of love, O King of peace"

Through the centuries Christians have voiced this cry from hearts wearied of war and dissension! "The wrath of sinful man restrain" is prayed fervently today when Satan has unleashed forces of evil to destroy homes; and nations are killing each other's young men. We call upon the Lord in desperation for the promise of the angels: "Glory to God in the highest, and on earth peace," they sang, "among men." Our Lord was born in humility and died in humility—manger and Cross symbolize His love for us. We can love each other only in His unselfish love; we can trust in Him only and the faithfulness of His Word.

God, give me disciplined faith—to trust in You and stand on Your promises, not the newspaper headlines. Amen.

SATURDAY, TWENTY-SIXTH WEEK
St. Matthew 8: 23-27.
"Eternal Father, strong to save"

We recall Jesus "whose voice the waters heard/And hushed their raging at thy word"; and the "Holy Spirit, who didst brood upon the chaos dark and rude,/And bid its angry tumult cease,/And give, for wild confusion, peace." Let us ask Jesus to still in our hearts the storms and wild confusion. We can sing this hymn in our "quiet time" as a prayer of protection for those in the armed services, members of the merchant marine and airlines; for all who travel.

Lord of the elements, I entrust all travelers to You; make us more aware of You than of dangers. Amen.

MONDAY, TWENTY-SEVENTH WEEK   I Peter 5: 8-11.
"We are soldiers of Christ, Who is mighty to save"

At baptism (as our hymn reminds us) "We are pledged to be faithful and steadfast and brave/Against Satan, the flesh, and the world." But most of us are rather undisciplined troops: we too often forget that "the armour we wear is Divine." By becoming so sophisticated, we have made it easier for the devil to find weak spots in our armour of faith. Christ has won the victory and He is winning it in our daily living: when we stand upon His promises, Satan has no power over us.

Thanks be to God who gives us victory in Jesus! Amen.

TUESDAY, TWENTY-SEVENTH WEEK
II Corinthians 12: 9-10.

"Jesus, my Saviour, look on me"

Rest, strength, light, peace, life are keynotes of each stanza of today's hymn and many of us may remember a time when that is what Jesus has meant to us. In dark nights of the soul, or under temptation by the enemy Satan, or wearied by the journey of life, we can come to Jesus and rest in Him, to be strengthened and led by His Grace into a new life lived in His Peace. "Living or dying" made no difference to St. Paul for Jesus was his all. Do we grit our teeth and stoically force our way in sheer willpower? Or do we learn the Saint's, secret of fixing our gaze on Jesus—letting His Cross bring victory!

Jesus, I trust You now to be "my all" in all things. Amen.

WEDNESDAY, TWENTY-SEVENTH WEEK
St. Matthew 14: 27.

"How firm a foundation"

A woman went to church with a heavy heart, facing a seemingly impossible task. Each thought in the service (from this opening hymn to the Psalms and Gospel reading) seemed to re-echo our Lord's words: "Take heart, it is I; have no fear." So this was the promise she had come to receive! She left that church as if she were a different person—healed of anxiety and worry, with new confidence! These words seemed to sing continuously in her heart: "The flame shall not hurt thee; I only design/Thy dross to consume, and thy gold to refine." By evening she could sing the last stanza in joyous assurance that Jesus would never forsake her or the loved one for whom she so earnestly prayed.

Jesus, help me to remain true to You while You win victory in my life. Amen.

THURSDAY, TWENTY-SEVENTH WEEK   Psalm 90: 1-4.
"O God, our help in ages past"

Our psalm reminds us that God brought forth the creation of the world and He is the same for all eternity. Since a thousand years are but as a day in His sight, we must not be impatient. God does not always protect us from suffering or trouble. He does not always remove our problems or temptations; for to do so would make us weaklings. But He answers our prayers with guidance, hope and help in this life—and "our eternal home" awaits us at the last. He transforms our extremities into opportunities for His love to be revealed.

God of mercy, help me today (as in the past) to withstand the blasts of life for You are my best comfort and defence. Amen.

FRIDAY, TWENTY-SEVENTH WEEK   Psalm 20: 7-9.
"God the Omnipotent! King, who ordainest"

This hymn and psalm praise God as all-powerful; but also all mercy and righteousness proceed from Him to us. If we really look to Him and *dwell in Him*—rather than in our own self-pity or fear—we will not be such "nervous Christians," singing hymns on Sunday and crowding psychiatrists' offices on Monday. If our moral fibre is based on faith in Him, rather than fear, we can pray for the heavy needs in the prayer list afforded by our daily newspaper. We can believe that God will give peace in His time.

Give peace, dear Father, to us Your wayward children and keep us faith-full to Your power and purposes. Amen.

SATURDAY, TWENTY-SEVENTH WEEK
St. Matthew 26: 41.

"I need thee every hour"

This refrain is better "background music" than most that we listen to daily. We need to come to our Saviour in joys as well as in sorrows and times of pain—to hear His Voice in the midst of life's temptations so that they will not have power over us. We are to "watch and pray" for there is often a subtle inner warfare between the willing spirit and the old habits and desires of the flesh. Too often people lean on cigarettes as a crutch and then wonder why they develop cancer. Jesus is *the answer* to all our needs! He can answer— even the need to heal a cancer.

Lord, help me to remember to lean on You (not a false prop) today. Amen.

MONDAY, TWENTY-EIGHT WEEK   Acts 3: 1-10.
"My faith looks up to thee"

The apostles Peter and John looked to Jesus and called upon His Name in faith—and the lame man walked! We are to be His modern apostles looking to Him to impart zeal and strength to our doubting minds and hearts. It is not faith in faith but *faith in Jesus,* who takes away our guilts and comforts our griefs. He removes our fears today when truly we look to Him—gazing on Him not on the problems or illnesses. His love for us is "Pure, warm and changeless . . . A living fire."

Jesus, use me to project Your faith not my fears, Your joy, not my sorrow; Your peace, not my anxiety today. Amen.

TUESDAY, TWENTY-EIGHTH WEEK   St. John 15: 9-10.
"More love to thee, O Christ"

When we are hurt by the world or our loved ones, the antidote to the poison is more love to Christ. The more we love Christ, the more we shall concern ourselves with His purposes (and less of our own except as His become ours). In a single verse of Scripture "abide in . . . love" is used three times. Are we dwelling in His love or dwelling on our own shortcomings, or those of others? To dwell in self-pity is to short circuit His joy; to dwell in anger is to separate ourselves from His love.

O, Christ, let this be my constant prayer: "More love to thee." Amen.

WEDNESDAY, TWENTY-EIGHTH WEEK
II Corinthians 1: 3-11.
"There's a wideness in God's mercy"

St. Paul emphasizes the mercy of God "who comforts us in all our affliction, so that we may be able to comfort those who are in any affliction." In verse 10 St. Paul says triumphantly, "he delivered us from so deadly a peril, and he will deliver us; on him we have set our hope that he will deliver us again." Clearly "the affliction we experienced in Asia" was a peril, not an illness! St. Paul was beaten, persecuted for his brave, unflinching witness. Many illnesses today are psychosomatic—not a result of persecution! Our hymn tells us "There is healing in his blood." Let's claim the "wideness in God's mercy" now so that we may be able to comfort others as He has comforted us.

God of mercy, in Your love forgive me and heal me so that I can be of more help to others. Amen.

THURSDAY, TWENTY-EIGHTH WEEK   James 1: 2-3.
"Go forward, Christian soldier"

There are ample warnings in Holy Scripture and many hymns to remind us that Jesus did not call us to a life of ease but rather to carry our share of His Cross. Like Him, we are engaged in spiritual warfare against forces of evil wherever we find them, even in our own homes. The severest of all testings is the scorn and bitterness of a husband or wife, parent or child who avowedly hates the Christ who must be Lord of a Christian's life! Sometimes the battle lasts so many years that the spirit seems to be faint in weariness, but our Lord knows the "... hourly need;/He can with bread of heaven/Thy fainting spirit feed."

Lord, help me not to fear the future of what any one can do to me for Your joy and love are my "secret weapons." Amen.

FRIDAY, TWENTY-EIGHTH WEEK   St. John 20: 11-18.
"I come to the garden alone"

Jesus appeared to Mary Magdalene at Easter in the garden; and like Mary, heartbroken and spiritually alone, we find we are *not* alone! Much as we prefer to evade "woe," often it is here that the Lord meets us most wonderfully. In despair, we stop trying to work out our own solutions, struggling against life. In our utter weakness, His strength can come into us! In submission, we stop screaming for our own way—long enough to hear His Voice showing us a better way. No one else can duplicate our experience. He has no favorites. Will you meet Him today in the garden of Gethsemane or of the Resurrection?

Jesus, come into the garden of my heart now and relieve my sorrow with Your peace. Amen.

SATURDAY, TWENTY-EIGHTH WEEK St. Matthew 11: 28.
"What a friend we have in Jesus"

His fiancee had drowned on the day before they were to be married and Joseph Scriven remained single, giving himself to good works and to the care of his mother, for whose comfort this hymn was written in a time of great sorrow. He knew Jesus as the Friend to whom he could turn in grief or temptation, in discouragement or pain, in weariness or loneliness. Do we? Or do we seek another person to bear our burdens? Or a crutch, like cigarettes or alcohol, which can even create new health problems! Do we forget the Friend of all friends?

Jesus, forgive me for trying to carry my own problems and needs instead of surrendering them to You. Give me Your comfort, Lord. Amen.

MONDAY, TWENTY-NINTH WEEK   I Corinthians 1: 4-9.
"Amazing grace! how sweet the sound"

Grace and praise are two words that should be linked together—so some add a chorus to this hymn: just one phrase repeated throughout, "Praise God". St. Paul gives thanks for God's grace which enriches Christian life with spiritual gifts and sustains those called into the fellowship of Jesus. Isn't it amazing that we often fail to accept this amazing grace which can turn the lost into the found? How wonderfully His grace can relieve our fears, protect us in dangers, and restore our sight—if only we have humility to invite Jesus to be our Saviour!

Lord, open my eyes now to see and praise Your grace at work within me. Amen.

TUESDAY, TWENTY-NINTH WEEK   St. John 6: 48-51.
Break Thou the bread of life"

Like the loaves and fishes brought by a small boy in Galilee, we can bring our lives to Jesus. At the service of Communion we are fed spiritually because He said: "I am the bread of life." He takes the brokenness of our lives, as we feed on Him through sacrament and Scripture, and heals and uses us to feed multitudes—if we are willing to let Him! He blesses the truth of sacrament and Scripture to our use and us to His service in sharing with others what we have received. He touches our eyes with His Holy Spirit to increase our sight spiritually and physically, when we seek *Him!*

Lord, enlighten me, feed me, heal me to Your glory. Amen.

WEDNESDAY, TWENTY-NINTH WEEK   James 1: 12-15.
"Yield not to temptation"

Temptation is not sin, but yielding to it is. Someone has said, "You can't keep the birds from flying over your head, but you can keep them from making nests in your hair!" Our Lord warned us of the devil's subtle tactics: the more committed we are to Jesus, the more subtly difficult they become! "The good is often the enemy of the best," warned Dr. E. Stanley Jones. We may be very busy doing good things, but if they are not our Lord's highest Will, we are *mis*-using time and talents. If we look to Jesus for help, He'll carry us through.

Jesus, prompt me to see the tempter's wiles; give me Your power to overcome his assaults and my weakness. Amen.

THURSDAY, TWENTY-NINTH WEEK   Romans 8: 31-34.
"Rock of ages, cleft for me"

The Church is intended to be the "household of God" built on the Rock of Christ Jesus. Our Lord, "who is at the right hand of God, who indeed intercedes for us," is the cornerstone: He will not fail us! As our hymn reminds us, we are very human saints in need of His divine Guidance, Pardon, Wisdom and Power. "Simply to thy cross I cling" reminds us of our frailty, our dependence on Jesus the Rock. It is a beautiful "sung-prayer" for us to become, by God's Grace, what we are intended to be. If we live dependent upon Him in this life, we need not fear death but will have the assurance of being with Him in glory! Our Scripture reminds us: "If God is for us, who is against us?"

Lord, heal our weaknesses, forgive our faithlessness and help us to overcome at last. Make us comforters of the broken in today's world even as You have already comforted us. Amen.

FRIDAY, TWENTY-NINTH WEEK   Romans 8: 35-39.
"Peace, perfect peace, in this dark world of sin"

Our peace is not dependent on circumstances but on our relationship with Jesus. If we believe that He is on the throne and that He has overcome the power of death and sin, we can trust in Him and find peace! When pressed by excessive burdens or sorrows, when alone or even facing death itself, we can have His peace. A friend, dying of terminal cancer, wrote in our Church bulletin: "I only know that I am one of the most fortunate persons in the world to be a part of the fellowship of this Church during a hazardous adventure like this. I do not know what the outcome will be; only that it will be triumphant, thanks to God's love and yours." Barbara's inner peace was radiant even in a shadowy body. We wanted her healed in this life—but we know that she was healed spiritually and that in glory she is rejoicing eternally! We grieved for ourselves, not for her. In the communion of saints, she is one with all of our church: praising the Lord in His perfect peace.

Jesus, keep us mindful that nothing can separate us from Your love and that in Your Will is our peace. Amen.

SATURDAY, TWENTY-NINTH WEEK   Hebrews 12: 1-2.
"Lo! what a cloud of witnesses"

This hymn, beautifully paraphrasing our Scripture, reminds us that in the communion of saints we are surrounded by "a cloud of witnesses"—those who have won the crown of eternal life. We are urged to lay aside sin as they did and run the race with perseverance in this life, so that in the life to come we may rejoice with the Father, Son and all the saints in the Church Triumphant. Jesus is the One to whom we look for salvation. But we can expect to rejoin our loved ones who in this life as baptised Christians confessed the Name of Jesus—and now are rejoicing in His Nearer Presence!

Lord, comfort me in the assurance that my loved ones are part of this cloud of witnesses. Amen.

MONDAY, THIRTIETH WEEK   I Kings 19: 11-12.
"Dear Lord and Father of mankind"

In this hymn the poet John Greenleaf Whittier echoes Elijah's experiences of nearly three thousand years ago! God is eternal—now and always. He is "Lord and Father of mankind." We need more than ever to pray ". . . Forgive our foolish ways!"/Reclothe us in our rightful mind,/In purer lives thy service find,/In deeper reverence, praise." Today's tensions increase the toll of ulcers and heart attacks. In the noise of life we need to hear God's "still, small voice"; we need to find His order and peace in our too heated striving. When we are too busy to pray and listen, we are bringing illness on ourselves.

Heavenly Father, forgive us for trying to live our lives in our own wisdom and strength. Speak to us today Your word of calm. Amen.

TUESDAY, THIRTIETH WEEK   St. Luke 7: 22-23.
"Thine arm, O Lord, in days of old"

We sing hymns about the healing touch of Jesus in Galilee but do we really expect His healing power to flow through the hands laid on us in faith today? Are we able to see in our church's sacraments the continuation of His ministry today? "And lo! thy touch brought life and health,/Gave speech, and strength, and sight." Do we smother the sick with pity or lift them in this sung-prayer: "And now, O Lord, be near to bless,/Almighty as of yore . . ./That whole and sick, and weak and strong,/May praise thee evermore."

Jesus, by faith I claim Your healing power: be glorified in me. Amen.

WEDNESDAY, THIRTIETH WEEK   Romans 5: 8.

"There is a green hill far away"

Our hearts bleed with our Lord on that first Good Friday as we sing this hymn reminding us that He died so we might be blessed, forgiven, saved from the retribution our sins deserve. No one else could pay this price that cost His life's blood for no one else was good enough—the Lamb without blemish. We don't have to get ourselves all cleaned up to go to God saying, "Look how good I am and all the good things I've done!" We can't make ourselves good, but we *can* "trust in the power of His redeeming blood" to redeem and free us from pride, resentments, jealousy — the sins that crucified Jesus.

Lord, help me now to forgive others as You have already forgiven me. Amen.

THURSDAY, THIRTIETH WEEK   I Peter 2: 24-25.

"Here, O my Lord, I see thee face to face"

At Communion we meet Jesus and give over to Him all our weariness, our burdens, our sins, our frailties of mind, body and soul. "He himself bore our sins in his body on the tree, that we might die to sin and live to righteousness." Our guilt for sins of omission or commission is washed away forever when we claim His righteousness instead of trying to justify ourselves by claiming our own. Then we can "taste afresh the calm of sin forgiven." As St. Peter wrote: "By his wounds you have been healed."

Jesus, heal me to Your glory. Amen.

FRIDAY, THIRTIETH WEEK   St. Mark 1: 9-13.

"Forty days and forty nights"

For many of us seeking to grow deeper in our relationship with God, this Scripture has been most comforting. Satan will press his temptations upon us but in Christ we shall not fall! Our Lord was tempted—immediately following His baptism. So shall we be—especially after some "mountaintop" experience. He fasted and prayed; and when Satan put before Him three temptations, Jesus did not dally with them as we so often do. He recognized the devil's efforts to distract Him from His main purposes of being the Saviour, the Living Bread, of winning men by love, of glorifying God.

Precious Saviour, be with us when Satan tempts us to doubt, fear or hate so that we may not succumb to his power but be released by Your saving power of love. Amen.

SATURDAY, THIRTIETH WEEK   I Corinthians 11: 23-32; St. Matthew 26: 26-28; St. Luke 24: 30-31.

"Come, risen Lord"

When we receive our Lord at Holy Communion we are actually asking Him to let us be *His guests*. We sing this modern hymn (1933) prayerfully remembering that it is at His holy table or altar that He manifests Himself to us in the Sacrament *He commanded:* "Do this in remembrance of me." We come not just as a memorial but rather for the *re-calling* of our Lord and by faith we accept the bread and the cup as if from His hands. "For as often as you eat this bread and drink the cup, you proclaim the Lord's death until he comes." (I Corinthians 11: 24, 26) As we receive Christ under the forms of bread and wine (or juice) we are one with saints of the past of all nations who have come in humility to His church, no matter what label it bears denominationally.

Jesus, I receive You in the way You made Yourself known to the disciples on the road to Emmaus: in the breaking of bread. Your Presence comforts and strengthens me now. Amen.

PART 5

Fruit of the Spirit

Most of us covet the fruit of the Spirit as St. Paul listed it in Galatians 5: 22-23: "love, joy, peace, patience, kindness, goodness, faithfulness, gentleness, self-control." Hopefully we ask God to give us this fruit, instead of asking Him to give us His indwelling Holy Spirit, *the Gift* Jesus promised to send after His Ascension! We ask for a grape instead of asking to be grafted into the grape vine so that we can be a branch, bearing desirable fruit (St. John 15: 5-6). We struggle along, withered branches, because we have not grasped the Truth and claimed the Answer. In Galatians 2: 20 St. Paul shares it with us: "I have been crucified with Christ; it is no longer I who live, but Christ who lives in me; and the life I now live in the flesh I live by faith in the Son of God, who loved me and gave himself for me."

Yes, by baptism we receive the Holy Spirit and in confirmation we pray for strengthening. Too often, though, we are like the unwise bishop who admonished the newly confirmed class: "But don't expect anything to happen." Jesus said before Pentecost that the Holy Spirit had been *with* the disciples but later *would be in them* (St. John 14: 16-17). Are you asking the Holy Spirit to be *in* you? *In full charge of your life* so that Jesus can give you *His* Power for living? Can you say with St. Paul: "Christ lives in me?" Bishop Stephen Bayne pointed outwisely in *Christian Living* that we are to let Jesus incarnate himself in each of us. As

Christians (Christ-ins) we will then bear the heavenly fruit of the Spirit. Let us meditate on this fruit and renew our commitment to Jesus. Let us ask that His Holy Spirit *possess us* to bring forth His fruit: *as we live in "fruit-bearing union" with Him*—daily!

Lord Jesus, incarnate Yourself in me so that I can fulfill Your highest purposes for my life. Keep me conscious of being part of the Vine so that Your fruit of the Spirit will be borne daily on the branch of my life. Help me to live throughout each day these sentence prayers: as a constant refrain in my spirit attuned to Your Holy Spirit. Amen.

MONDAY, THIRTY-FIRST WEEK   St. John 3: 16.

God revealed Himself to us in Jesus to show us His Nature of love lived out in humanity. The Incarnation is God in the flesh of man. Jesus was as much of God as could be revealed in and to man—God entering into human life in the Person of Jesus so that we might better know Him whom we worship. Jesus revealed God's Will perfectly in His earthly ministry of healing all in need.

Lord, help me today to see You more clearly, love You more completely and follow You more closely. Amen.

TUESDAY, THIRTY-FIRST WEEK

St. Luke 5: 12-16; St. John 10: 30 (NEB).
Jesus said, "My Father and I are one." God's Will is expressed not only in the teaching but in the life of Jesus. Not counting the events of the last week, two-thirds of the Gospel accounts are stories of His healing ministry. Whenever He saw human need, the love of Jesus flowed out to heal it. His words, His touch made people whole in mind, body and soul. His healing power can be released in us today, for His Will has not changed.

Lord, I accept Your healing Will thankfully today. Amen.

WEDNESDAY, THIRTY-FIRST WEEK   Romans 6: 5-11.

Jesus revealed God's Will not only in His Life but through His Resurrection He gave us the power to live according to His Will. When we realize our own helplessness and our need for a Saviour, we can turn to him and be saved: His death released the power to overcome! When we die to our own self-will, He transforms our wills according to our needs and His Will. His power becomes effective in our lives: we are reborn into a right relationship!

Lord, help me to die unto self, living unto Jesus. Amen.

THURSDAY, THIRTY-FIRST WEEK   Revelation 3: 20-22.

When we give ourselves to Jesus, He is able to give Himself more fully to us. He stands at the door of our hearts and knocks, waiting for us to open and give Him room to live in us. He accepts even a crack, but the wider we open to Him, the more He can give of Himself to us. This is the Greatest Gift we can receive, the indwelling of the Holy Comforter (Strengthener) who is God the Holy Spirit, manifesting Himself in us.

Blessed Jesus, live in me through Your Holy Spirit today. Amen.

FRIDAY, THIRTY-FIRST WEEK   Romans 12: 1.

Jesus manifested God to the world. As we approach Epiphany, we see the world (Gentiles) represented by the Wise Men bringing gifts. The gift of incense is our loving worship; the gift of gold is our stewardship of money and resources and talents; the gift of myrrh is our suffering which is not bitter when offered to Jesus to be redeemed and transformed. These represent the gift of ourselves, the *only* gift we can really make to God!

Lord, I give myself to You. Amen.

SATURDAY, THIRTY-FIRST WEEK
St. John 15: 12-17, 26.

In the manifestation of Christ to the world we have a part. If we are letting His Holy Spirit live in us, a radiance that is not ours will be manifested in and through us. His light will be enkindled within our hearts, His Spirit of love will be incarnated within us, showing forth in all our words and deeds. We shall be instruments of His peace, bringers of joy, patient and kind, gentle and good, faithful and self-controlled.

Jesus, manifest Yourself in me to bless others. Amen.

MONDAY, THIRTY-SECOND WEEK   Galatians 5: 22-23.
The Holy Spirit is given to us in Baptism. The seed has been planted; but just as an apple seed does not produce apples overnight, so the fruit of the Spirit is not instantly matured. We are given this gift that He may grow in us day by day, changing us, bringing forth the fruit of love, joy, peace, patience, kindness, goodness, faithfulness, gentleness and self-control.

Lord, bring forth the fruit of the Spirit within me. Amen.

TUESDAY, THIRTY-SECOND WEEK   Romans 8: 11.
All of us need healing. None of us can claim perfection of the body—how often illness comes unannounced! Neither can we claim perfection of the mind: we need more of the mind that was in Christ Jesus—to think His thoughts. Least of all can we claim perfection of the soul lest we be guilty of spiritual pride. When we consciously accept the gift of the Holy Spirit, allowing Him to work His Will in us, we find divine healing.

Lord, thank You for the gift of Your Holy Spirit. Amen.

WEDNESDAY, THIRTY-SECOND WEEK
Galatians 5: 24-25.

A woman was healed of blindness when she stopped badger-

ing God in her prayers for her sight to be restored and trust-
fully asked Him to give her whatever was His best gift. Inner
peace preceded sight! Too often God cannot give us His Highest Gift because we are clamouring childishly for a lesser one.
Our greatest need is for the Holy Spirit to reign in us: this is
the basis for true healing.

Lord, help me to make Your Holy Spirit the ruler of my life.
Amen.

THURSDAY, THIRTY-SECOND WEEK   St. John 15: 1-5.
When we ask God to stir up the gift of the Holy Spirit within
us, He may give us opportunities to use the gift. He may
show us where to let His love and kindness ripen in our lives,
or where we need to let His gentleness and goodness mature.
He may want us to let His joy dispel our sorrow or His peace
replace our tension.

Lord, let the fruit of Your Holy Spirit ripen in me today.
Amen.

FRIDAY, THIRTY-SECOND WEEK
Romans 8: 26-30 and Ephesians 3: 8.
These are the "unsearchable riches of Christ," the treasure
money cannot buy. This is the mystery that we who are
unworthy can be so transformed by His worthiness. This is
divine healing that in our sickness of mind, body and soul His
Holy Spirit can penetrate to our deepest need, giving us the
virtue to correct our lack, manifesting in us the power of
God. Healing without the inner growth of the Holy Spirit is
seldom permanent: if the cause is not corrected, another out-
break occurs.

Heal me within, Lord, by the increase of Your Holy Spirit.
Amen.

SATURDAY, THIRTY-SECOND WEEK   Hebrews 12: 1-2.

Walking in the Spirit, we are to lay aside every weight—the special sins that beset us most easily. It is well to be honest with ourselves and with God. If we are carrying the heavy weight of fears or resentments, we need to confess them to God and then lay them aside, looking unto Jesus. When our eyes are fixed on Him and His forgiveness of us, we shall not be angry over what someone has done to hurt us.

Jesus, love . . . (Name) . . . through me; then love me through her or him. Amen.

MONDAY, THIRTY-THIRD WEEK   I Corinthians 13: 1-8.

Love is the antidote for hate, anger, grudge-holding, resentment, jealousy. It has been truly said, "If love doesn't work, increase the dosage." To walk in the Spirit, we must reach up in faith to Christ with one hand and out in love to our fellows with the other. Divine healing flows into us through faith and out of God's love to others. If we do not allow the outflowing of His love through us as a channel, we are not apt to receive much of the inflowing.

Lord, make me a channel of Your love today. Amen.

TUESDAY, THIRTY-THIRD WEEK   I John 4: 7-13.

An elderly woman, almost ninety, was healed of partial deafness. When asked how it happened, she said, "I just went every week to Holy Communion praying for God to heal all the sick. One day I realized that people were talking too loudly!" In love she had gone faithfully to be a channel of God's blessing to other sick ones; and in His mercy, God poured His healing power into ears that needed hearing. In love she had continually obeyed His Voice.

Lord, open my ears to hear Your Voice—today. Amen.

WEDNESDAY, THIRTY-THIRD WEEK

St. John 15: 18-21.

When our love is tested under the fire of unjust criticism, or outright opposition to what we are sure is God's Will, we are bearing Christ's Cross. This is Christian suffering—not the physical pain that is a result of our own petty anger or grudges, but the pain that comes from seeing His love rejected. When we walk with Jesus, His light shining through us may make the shadows deeper—but He is there in His love to heal and bless!

Father, forgive them for they know not what they do. Amen.

THURSDAY, THIRTY-THIRD WEEK   Ephesians 3: 14-21.

A Christian without love is as effective as a watch without a mainspring or an automobile without an engine. We are to walk in the love of Jesus, accepting Him as our Lord, the Mainspring of our lives, the motive Power. Our own human love is not enough and we are told to walk not in that but in Him—hearing, believing, obeying and letting His love flow through us. "Looking, longing, loving, we become like Him."

Jesus, let Your love reign in me today. Amen.

FRIDAY, THIRTY-THIRD WEEK   Ephesians 4: 1-3.

If our hearts are filled to overflowing with the Love of Christ —in active goodwill, not passive—our dispositions will be loving. We shall be able to love the unlovely and unlovable because Christ died for us while we, too, were yet sinners. When we let His Spirit bear fruit in us, we love the sinner enough to be Christ's redemptive channel for healing, aware of our own need still. We must be willing to love unceasingly with no exceptions—to be *part of the answer* to our prayers!

Lord, make me a channel of blessing today. Amen.

SATURDAY, THIRTY-THIRD WEEK

James 1: 2-8; 12-18.

After singing the Passover hymn, Jesus and His disciples went out to the Mount of Olives. We, too, can face our greatest tests if we go into the night singing to lift our spirits. "Hymning our way to heaven" is not a bad idea. "On our way rejoicing" is the spirit of the Christian facing trouble, pain, loss—for in our need our Lord's Presence can be most real and from our testing can come a more deeply rooted faith.

Lord, give me Your joy in my testings today. Amen.

MONDAY, THIRTY-FOURTH WEEK

I Peter 1: 6-9 (NEB).

God does not allow testings without a purpose. We are to pray for deliverance, healing, knowing that in the right way and place and time God will bring good out of trials, used by Him to strengthen us. Jesus is revealed to us in the proving of our faith: in victory through His power! But His joy sustains us even as we pass through the "fire" because we *know* that He will bring the blessing, the "harvest of your faith."

Thank You, Lord, that Your Holy Spirit brings me healing joy, even in this testing. Amen.

TUESDAY, THIRTY-FOURTH WEEK

St. John 16: 19-24.

Jesus authorized us to pray in His Name so that our joy might be complete. In the Bible, a name often denotes the person's nature. When we take the Name of Jesus into our prayers we are also to take *His Nature,* tailoring our prayers accordingly. We can then expect to receive a joyous answer when we pray truly in the Name of Jesus. If we are living in Him and He in us, our prayers will be prayed in His Name and power.

Lord, thank You for Your abiding joy. Amen.

WEDNESDAY, THIRTY-FOURTH WEEK
St. John 15: 11-17.

Asking in Jesus' Name implies *obedience* to His commands to love one another as He has loved us. The unloving person is never one in whom the joy of Jesus wells up and overflows. Prayers, it is said, travel on two "wings": love and joy. If we lack joy, we do well to look for our point of lack of love which is disobedience to our Lord. Joy is one of the marked fruit that bears witness to our Lord's indwelling Presence.

Lord, let Your joy flood me today. Amen.

THURSDAY, THIRTY-FOURTH WEEK
Nehemiah 8: 10.

"Christian Joy is the result of a clear conscience," the mark of obedience. Sin not only takes away our joy but it costs us our strength in the Lord. It is the most expensive luxury! We can't afford separation from God because of some unconfessed sin for which we have not accepted His forgiving, healthy love. Guilt lies behind many diseases but Christians have no right to harbor guilt when they can be forgiven, transformed by the joy of the Lord.

Father, forgive me and give me Your Joy. Amen.

FRIDAY, THIRTY-FOURTH WEEK
I John 1: 3-4.

Jesus did not die for our sins so that we should shuffle along with burdens of guilt. "He died that we might be forgiven, /He died to make us good."* Our response is to make ourselves a living sacrifice to Jesus, our Saviour. The gladdest saints have been those who found their joy in naming all as Christ's. "Jesus first, others next, yourself last = JOY." When we concentrate on giving joy to God and others, not ourselves, we are being healed.

Make me Your channel of hope and joy, Lord, today. Amen.

* Quoted from the hymn "There is a Green Hill Far Away" by C. F. Alexander.

SATURDAY, THIRTY-FOURTH WEEK
II Thessalonians 3: 16.

"Peace of the heart is that tranquility of the spirit that lends a halo," someone has said. The angels proclaimed this peace; and through His healing touch, Jesus brought peace to the minds, bodies and souls of those in need. The gift of His Spirit brings peace, deep blessedness, to those who yearn for and accept this crown of life. Peace is more than the absence of trouble or pain: often, when lifted to Him, He gives us peace by these very means!

Lord, increase in me Your healing peace today. Amen.

MONDAY, THIRTY-FIFTH WEEK   Psalm 23: 2.

Often we rebel against God because of some illness that we have brought on ourselves by breaking His laws, natural (physical) or spiritual. No one is immune to the unfortunate results of disobeying God's laws—but His forgiveness can make the experience of illness a lying down in green pastures beside still waters. Often we will not listen to God's Voice except in the quiet of an enforced rest. In our much busyness, we forget to listen; in His forgiving-ness, we are at peace.

Lord, fill me with peace—Your peace. Amen.

TUESDAY, THIRTY-FIFTH WEEK   Isaiah 26: 3.

Many of us are so busy hurrying about that we haven't time to accept God's peace. If our minds are really stayed on Him, we shall know which things He intends for us to do and how they can best be accomplished. During a sudden storm while crossing the bay in a sailboat, the stay broke—but the young skipper prayed for strength to hold his sail. His mind was stayed on God and he came safely into port.

Lord, be my Mainstay in all the storms today. Amen.

WEDNESDAY, THIRTY-FIFTH WEEK   Isaiah 30: 15.

To work most effectively for God, we must take time to absorb some of His peace. When our nerves are frazzled, we make costly mistakes, wearing out our bodies unnecessarily. When we start the day with a "quiet time," God's healing peace sinks deeply into our subconscious minds (called the "heart" in the Bible). If filled with God's peace, the "heart" is strong in the midst of trial, calm and tranquil in spite of strife, healed in time of pain.

God, make me tranquil in Your peace in spite of strife. Amen.

THURSDAY, THIRTY-FIFTH WEEK   St. John 14: 27.

Jesus bequeathed His peace to those who receive the baptism of the Holy Spirit. This Gift is not one the world can give—no money can buy such a blessing! The peace that is a fruit of the Spirit banishes fear and sets troubled minds to rest. It is the peace that passes understanding. Those who possess it have the pearl of great price, the Kingdom of Heaven within them. Healing often comes when this peace rules our hearts.

Lord, reign in me today, granting me Your Peace. Amen.

FRIDAY, THIRTY-FIFTH WEEK   I Peter 5: 14.

Belonging to Christ wholly, not halfheartedly, is the secret of inner peace. Our strivings cease inwardly as we commit ourselves fully and solely to His Way, not our own or another's. Wanting only His Will, we can accept whatever comes to us in life, content that He will use and transform it to our highest good, no matter what it may be. Such peace is possible, even in this world, when our eyes are focused on the Cross, not ourselves.

In Your Will is my peace, Lord Jesus. Amen.

SATURDAY, THIRTY-FIFTH WEEK   Romans 15: 5-7.
Patience is a fruit of the Spirit we often find difficult to
cultivate unless we remind ourselves constantly of our Lord's
patience with us. We, too, nail our Lord to the Cross! Often
when we pray for patience, God gives us opportunities to
practice it. If we feel impatient because of disagreeable traits
of others, we do well to remind ourselves that the feeling
may be mutual. Some psychiatrists say we criticize in others
the sin we hate secretly in ourselves.

Lord, let me see others through Your eyes today. Amen.

MONDAY, THIRTY-SIXTH WEEK   I Peter 2: 18-25.
Sometimes we learn patience through Christian suffering—
when we are accused unjustly and suffer for righteousness,
"because God is first in our thoughts." This undeserved suffering is the true bearing of the Cross. We "follow in his
steps" when we suffer for sins we have not committed and
refuse to fight back at unjust accusations. We must beware of
any trace of pride in martyrdom. A servant is not better than
his master: as Christ was persecuted, so we may be also.

Lord, I'll follow You. Help me to be faith-full. Amen.

TUESDAY, THIRTY-SIXTH WEEK
                    I Peter 3: 13-18, and St. Luke 13: 16.
Sickness may be a means by which we learn patience: sufferers from arthritis may be more patient with fellow sufferers. But this does *not mean that God intentionally wills
the sickness* in order to develop the fruit of patience! Suffering for our faith provides ample opportunities for maturing
patience! Jesus healed the disease of the woman "whom Satan had bound." If God brings good out of sin or evil, it does
not mean He wills or *sends* either; rather, He is not defeated!

Help me to be patient, God. Amen.

WEDNESDAY, THIRTY-SIXTH WEEK

Colossians 3: 12-14.

Patience has been called the outer garment and kindness the inner garment. If we are genuinely kind in our hearts, we can easily be patient in our relationships with others. Kindness stems from our love of Jesus, our Lord and Master, whose love we share with our fellow men. Human love alone is not apt to be consistently kind and patient. Divine love lifts the human to the sublime; the Spirit indwelling bears these fruit.

Lord, may Your Holy Spirit make me more kind today to everyone I meet. Amen.

THURSDAY, THIRTY-SIXTH WEEK

I Peter 3: 8-9 (NEB).

Being "full of brotherly affection, kindly" is an attribute of a Christian—or should be, but can we honestly claim this fruit? Do we treat everyone with the kindliness we would show to our most beloved brother? Are our churches known for kindness to the stranger, the one of another race, the socially less acceptable? If our kindness is only skindeep, we are falling short of the measure of Jesus Christ. We may also find ourselves in need of healing!

Lord, make me Your channel of kindness today. Amen.

FRIDAY, THIRTY-SIXTH WEEK   II Peter 1: 5-8 (NEB).

Faith, virtue, knowledge, self-control, fortitude, piety are all most desirable—but the Christian life is not complete without brotherly kindness and love. We must not only receive these gifts but must foster or cultivate them until they come to possess us. When possessed by the spirit of kindness, we shall not be critical. Jesus will open many doors where we can mediate our gift! If we lack this fruit, we have forgotten how very kind Jesus has been to us.

Lord, make kindness my watchword today. Amen.

SATURDAY, THIRTY-SIXTH WEEK

St. Matthew 5: 1-12.

"If we are hungry enough for the fullness of the Spirit, we shall be filled." Most of us want the fruit of the Spirit, but we are not desperate enough! When we are ready to say "What would Jesus do?"—and do it—guidance and power will come. God does not delay: we keep Him waiting. We fail to let the Holy Spirit dwell in our hearts. His blessed attitudes can change our petty ones until we are filled with the goodness of God.

Holy Spirit, make me a child of God today. Amen.

MONDAY, THIRTY-SEVENTH WEEK   St. Mark 9: 15-29.

Evelyn Underhill has said that "consecration in overalls" is faithfulness. It is to continue steadily in the work assigned to us no matter what conditions exist. We are to put our trust in God, casting on Him whatever burdens, tempts or grieves us. As we look unto Jesus, the Author and Finisher of our faith, He will answer our every need. We are to fix our eyes on Him, not the pain or the medicine, expectantly claiming His promises for healing.

Thank You, Lord, that You are always faithful to Your promises. Amen.

TUESDAY, THIRTY-SEVENTH WEEK

St. Mark 11: 22-24.

"I refuse to be disappointed; I will only praise" is our best attitude. We must do *more* than believe that God may heal us or that He has the power to do so. Expectancy means claiming the blessing, counting upon it, going forward in faith, reckoning upon it, confessing it and acting "within the conditions of the answered prayer." It means abiding in Christ, not the disease, accepting the Lordship of the indwelling Holy Spirit to lift us above bondage to fear.

Lift me to Your Presence. Amen.

WEDNESDAY, THIRTY-SEVENTH WEEK

I Peter 2: 11-22.

Goodness is not mere pleasantness, being a "goody-good," not just correct moral behavior, "living by the law," or being a "do-gooder." True goodness is not anything we can attain of ourselves; it is a reflection of the Lord's goodness which shines out through our lives as "we dwell in Him and He in us." As we receive Him in Holy Communion, His Holy Spirit is strengthened in us so that we are fortified to go back into the market place of life.

Lord, may Your goodness change me today. Amen.

THURSDAY, THIRTY-SEVENTH WEEK

St. Matthew 19: 16-26.

This does not permit us to evade God's commandments. It does mean we cannot live by the letter of the law as the Pharisees were doing. True goodness is a fruit of *full commitment*, being willing to give up money, prestige or whatever false gods we worship more than God so that we may respond *fully* to His call to *obedience*! True divine healing is accompanied by consecration of life. We give ourselves wholeheartedly to God's demands, laying aside other lesser loves.

Lord, what do You want me to do? Amen.

FRIDAY, THIRTY-SEVENTH WEEK   I Peter 2: 1-5.

We are to lay aside dishonesty (when we don't want to see someone or talk on the telephone); malice (repeating anything that is not kind and good about others, regardless of its truth); pretence (false humility as well as false affections of goodness); jealousy (praying for enough humility to love the victim of our envy); recrimination (not letting God alone be the Judge while we walk in the Spirit as peacemakers). We must pray for God's right-useness of our lives.

Lord, help me to do as You would do today. Amen.

SATURDAY, THIRTY-SEVENTH WEEK   I Peter 3: 3-4.

Gentleness (humility in some translations) is not a showy fruit of the indwelling Holy Spirit yet its omission is one of the telltale signs that our fruit is of self, not of Him. If we can fit quietly into God's Plan, humbly accepting with gentleness whatever He brings to us, being self-forgetful not self-assertive, then the Spirit is really bearing fruit in us. A great mystic, a Mistress of Theology, left as her dying message: "Make yourselves small, very small."

Lord, let me decrease that You may increase. Amen.

MONDAY, THIRTY-EIGHTH WEEK
II Timothy 2: 22-26; and St. Luke 23: 34.

God is more concerned that we grow the fruit of the Spirit than that we carry out some of our own flamboyant plans of work for Him. When the fruit of gentleness has matured in us, it is amazing how much more He can do through us than in our zealously self-assertive stages. Forbearing and forgiving releases greater power than resisting! Jesus saved the world in His prayer, "Father, forgive them; for they know not what they do." Who are we to do otherwise?

Father, forgive us for our unforgiving-ness. Amen.

TUESDAY, THIRTY-EIGHTH WEEK   Philippians 4: 13.

Self-control is the last named and one of the hardest fruits to mature in us. For the Christian, self-control is really surrender to the Lordship or control of Jesus. Only by daily study of His Will, seeking to be like Him, can we make our dedication really effective. As His control increases in us, His victory brings us deep, abiding joy. When He has won the victory over our self-assertiveness, we can appropriate all that He has: joy, strength, purity, patience, love.

Jesus, be All in all of me always. Amen.

WEDNESDAY, THIRTY-EIGHT WEEK

Colossians 2: 6-8.

Most people think self-control is rigidity, reserve, pushing down one's feelings to conform to moral or social codes. The self-control that is the fruit of the Holy Spirit is release of our own rigidities, loyalties and wills to God's control. It is not a pushing down of our true feelings, but rather a lifting up to Jesus who alone can bring our true natures under His control of perfect love! It is not reserve but willingness to let *Him* control.

Jesus, dictate what I shall think, say and do today. Amen.

THURSDAY, THIRTY-EIGHT WEEK

Philippians 2: 12-13.

A nervous breakdown often results when a person tries to push down strong fears or resentments instead of facing them in the light and love of Christ who gives His power to over-come. Healing begins when we face these emotions one by one, bringing them out in the open, examining them, con-fessing them to God as lack of faith or love, asking forgive-ness and leaving them in His hands. God in mercy works His healing within us.

Lord, cleanse me and heal me, renewing in me Your spirit of love. Amen.

FRIDAY, THIRTY-EIGHT WEEK   Galatians 2: 19-21.

When all our ambitions, yearnings and loves are under the control of Jesus, our words, attitudes and decisions will re-flect the Lord's abiding Presence in us. St. Paul, knowing his spirit was being brought under the control of Jesus, wrote: I live—but it is really no longer the same "I" who used to dominate my body, for now the Spirit of Jesus abides in me (paraphrase). Faith in Jesus controlled his life, not fearful obedience to Jewish law.

Christ Jesus, live in me today. Amen.

SATURDAY, THIRTY-EIGHTH WEEK
II Timothy 1: 6-10.

The Holy Spirit is given to us so that we may renew Him in our hearts—to bring us to repentance when we sin against God's Will, to create in us a right spirit and a new heart. In the process of being changed in our deepest inner desires and set free from bondage to our buried fears or hates, we are transformed by the power of the Holy Spirit. We are to touch the hem of Christ's garment and be healed in mind, body and soul. We shall never be the same, thank God!

Touch me and heal me, Lord, today. Amen.

MONDAY, THIRTY-NINTH WEEK   Acts 1: 8; 2: 1-4.

Before Pentecost, Peter was a weak, squeamish coward; James and John were squabbling for the best seats; Thomas was a rank doubter. After they had received the full baptism of the Holy Spirit, they were changed into powerful channels of God's healing love: fearless before martyrdom, confident and joyous in time of trouble. There is no limit to what God can do through the life that has become an aperture (or channel) for the outpouring of His Holy Spirit in selfless love.

Lord, make me a channel usable for Your purposes today. Amen.

TUESDAY, THIRTY-NINTH WEEK   Ephesians 4: 13-16.

We need spiritual feeding daily if we are going to grow into the full stature of Christ. We, the Church, the Body of Christ, of which He is the Head, need to be built up in love, bonded and knit together, the whole dependent upon each member. We need to pray daily for each other for the stirring up of the Spirit within us that we may bear fruit, bringing glory to His Name. We need to be healed by Him, within and without, as witness to His power.

Lord, help me to witness in my daily life to Your Spirit. Amen.

WEDNESDAY, THIRTY-NINTH WEEK   Romans 8: 5-19.
As the Spirit indwells us, we are motivated not of hate but of
love; not of sorrow but of joy; not of tension but of peace;
not of impatience but of patience; not of judgment but of
kindness; not of retaliation but of goodness; not of fear but
of faith-fullness; not of harshness but of gentleness; not of
selfishness but controlled by Christ Himself. God's ways are
not our ways: they are simpler, better. His thoughts are not
ours: they are deeper, higher.

Make me wholly Thine, O Lord. Amen.

THURSDAY, THIRTY-NINTH WEEK   St. John 15: 7-8.
Sanctification (fruit-bearing) is the working out *daily* of the
experience of the Cross—the indwelling Jesus—in *all* our relationships. If we become preoccupied with watching the fruit
grown in us, we shall take our eyes off Jesus. Preoccupation
with self destroys the Kingdom of Jesus. Being made into His
image is a lifetime's work and none of us has arrived.

Lord, help me to keep my eyes on You and not on the fruit
You are bearing in me. Help me to be patient but not com-
placent as You work out Your Will in my life to Your glory.
Amen.

FRIDAY, THIRTY-NINTH WEEK   St. John 15: 16.
Isn't it comforting to realize that Jesus has chosen us and
appointed for us to bear fruit—lasting fruit? When we feel
most inadequate, even a failure in our own eyes, we may be
bearing fruit to *His* liking. If we are continuing obediently to
love in difficult situations, He may be whispering to us:
"When you think you've done the least, I have been able to
do the most, through you."

Thank You, Jesus for Your comfort. Thank You for choosing
me for this difficult love-assignment. Amen.

SATURDAY, THIRTY-NINTH WEEK   James 3: 17-18

Our Scripture reminds us that "the harvest of righteousness is sown in peace by those who make peace." If we plant seeds of discord, we shall reap the same. If we make peace, we are sowing seeds that will bring the fruit of right-useness in our lives—and ultimately in the lives of those about us. It will truly take "wisdom from above" at times of stress. By our lives we shall be used to make Jesus known to others. As they see the fruit of the Spirit in us, they will seek the same Saviour we have found. We are to be "reproducers" not of ourselves, but of His heavenly fruit. Those, who (having tasted of ours) have come for themselves to the same Vine, will be the new crop.

Lord Jesus, let the fruit in my life draw others to be grafted into the Vine in fruit-bearing union. Amen.

PART 6

Gifts of the Spirit

We have been meditating on the fruit of the Spirit, always remembering that fruit is borne on the branch that is grafted into the Vine (St. John 15: 4). We can grow fruit of patience and love and all the rest—even if we do not ask Jesus to give us the gifts of the Holy Spirit. But we will be forfeiting not only blessings but *opportunities for service* if we do not *ask and accept His highest gifts*! At the same time we invite the Holy Spirit to possess us in fruit-bearing union, we need to ask Him to give us His supernatural gifts for power to live victoriously to His glory in our all-too-troubled world. We may have some abilities in teaching, preaching, etc., *before* we receive the baptism in the Holy Spirit, but afterwards, the work is done *through* us in greater effectiveness and with greater ease!

These gifts are given not for selfish purposes but so that we may be (1) led into all truth (St. John 14: 16, 17); (2) bear witness to Jesus (St. John 15: 26); (3) glorify Him (St. John 16: 14). These gifts are not for self-glorification of the individual (or glorification—idolatry—by others of the one being used by the Lord) but for the building up of His Body the Church to the Lord's glory!

The Gift of the Holy Spirit is more important than any of the gifts (or manifestations, as some prefer to term them). But until Pentecost the disciples were powerless in the face of skepticism and real persecution. After Pentecost they were changed because they could expect the Holy Spirit to give them the manifestations *as needed*: wisdom, knowledge, faith, gifts of healing, miracles, prophecy, the ability to distinguish between spirits, various kinds of tongues and the interpretation of tongues. "All these are inspired by one and the same Spirit, who apportions to each one individually as he wills" (I Corinthians 12: 11). The Third Person of the Trinity, *The Holy Spirit, will give us the gifts when He chooses to use us.* Do we will to be chosen? Do we will to receive? Let us ask ourselves daily these two questions as we meditate on the gifts of the Spirit.

Come, Holy Spirit, anoint me with Your gifts of power for ministry to Your glory: in my home, my church and my community. Give me wisdom to know Your Will, a deeper knowledge of Jesus and the discernment to make the right choices in my daily living. Give me each gift as I need it so that in my inadequacy Your power can be effective. Use me to minister to Your other children as You choose, when You choose. Glorify Yourself through my life. Amen.

MONDAY, FORTIETH WEEK   I Corinthians 12: 4-7.
St. Paul wrote that the gifts of the Spirit are manifestations
of the Holy Spirit given to each for the common good, i.e.,
for the building up of the church, "the body of Christ." The
interdependence of members of the church is symbolized by
the parts of the human body; when one part is sick the whole
body is weakened. Like St. Paul, we need to seek the *higher*
gifts if we are to be effective in the Lord's work. If the early
church needed supernatural wisdom, or knowledge and healing powers, so do we today. Far too many are *un*informed or
*mis*informed: they lack God's power to live victoriously because they do not ask!

Come into me, Holy Spirit, and fill me; saturate me like a
sponge, with Your Spirit. Make me more usable today.
Amen.

TUESDAY, FORTIETH WEEK   I Corinthians 12: 7, 11-13.
The Holy Spirit manifests Himself in each of us for the fulfillment of *His purposes*—but *all* of the gifts come from the
same Source. They are given for the edification and empowering of the individual so that he or she may be a more
effective member of Christ's Body the Church. The danger is
not in the use of any or all of the gifts when the recipient's
sole purpose is to glorify Jesus; the danger is that self-glorification may seep into the situation. The gifts are usually needed in combination and the individual often does not ask specifically for any one gift but rather that the Holy Spirit give
him *all the gifts needed to minister in a situation.*

Come, Holy Spirit, and purify me. Make me an instrument
You can use. Give me the gifts, as You choose, that will make
me more effective in Your service. Amen.

WEDNESDAY, FORTIETH WEEK

I Corinthians 12: 27-28.

Some of us may be needed as teachers, some as modern prophets, some as channels of God's healing power and still others as administrators. The indwelling Holy Spirit is needed by us all, but He may manifest Himself in each of us in different ways at different times. Many today, like St. Paul, are blessed with *all* the gifts, probably because they seek *all* that God wants to give them—in humility, acknowledging Him as the Giver of all good gifts! Some *limit* God's generosity by prejudice or fear, being unwilling to accept *all* that He yearns to give.

Lord, make me so empty of self that I may be ready and willing to receive *all* Your gifts today. Amen.

THURSDAY, FORTIETH WEEK   I Corinthians 12: 8-11.

The manifestations of the Holy Spirit are listed by St. Paul in our Scripture as wisdom, knowledge, faith, gifts of healing, miracles, prophesy, discernment of spirits, gift of tongues, and the interpretation of tongues. In the ministry of divine healing, at one time or another all of these gifts are helpful. In the ministry of preaching, certainly the first three are needed as well as prophecy at times. For a teacher, the same gifts are needed as well as a discernment of spirits, to know which is the true seeker and which a tool of Satan. The devil uses people to distract a meeting with "red herrings." In counseling, various if not all the gifts are needed for effective ministry.

Lord Jesus, give me through Your Holy Spirit whatever gifts I need today to serve You best. Amen.

FRIDAY, FORTIETH WEEK   I Corinthians 12: 8-11.

For the individual there is always the "ministry of intercession," even though not all are teachers or preachers. We need to *pray more for each other* and these gifts can help us to do so more *effectively*! We need to ask for wisdom to know how to pray in God's understanding (not our own myopic sight). We need a deeper knowledge of *His* purposes for other people as well as ourselves. Too often we try to superimpose our own human ideas or solutions on another. We need faith to believe even *before we see the answer—*to *expect* a miracle and to *accept* it when it happens! How often those around a person will not accept the healing or transformation after it has occurred and they *hold back God's victory* in the one *being* healed.

God give me wisdom, knowledge, faith and an expectancy to pray for and accept the miracle when it happens. Amen.

SATURDAY, FORTIETH WEEK   James 4: 3-8; 1: 5

If we need wisdom we are to ask God for it. We need to know *how* to pray. Many times we do not receive because we "pray amiss" in the wrong spirit or the wrong way. If our request is not God's will, then we should discern this from the beginning and ask Him to show us what is His Will in the situation. After we have discerned His Will, we are to pray *single-mindedly with faith—*not haphazardly in double-mindedness! Let us learn to *listen*, to claim the power of the Blood of Jesus over distracting "inner voices" of the subconscious or the insinuations of the enemy. We are to *resist the devil* and his distractions, confusions, accusations. We are to come closer to God and let *His Wisdom* guide us into His Truth.

Heavenly Father, give me Your gift of wisdom today through the indwelling Holy Spirit, so that I may pray and act according to Your highest Will. Amen.

MONDAY, FORTY-FIRST WEEK   St. John 8: 31-36.

We need to pray for the gift of knowledge. Jesus said that we must continue in His Truth, if we would be His disciples. It is His Truth—the knowledge or understanding of it—that will set us free from human bondages. Like Jews who at once claimed indignantly that they were "Abraham's descendants," we too claim to be Anglicans (or Episcopalians), Methodists, Presbyterians, Baptists. We can thank God for the nurturing of our churches. But it is the knowledge of the Truth (which the Holy Spirit gives us) that makes us vitally aware of Jesus. It is the Son of God who sets us free! He can free us from bondages in the past as well as present; and from fear of the future.

Holy Spirit, lead me into deeper knowledge of Jesus who died to set me free. Help me to know this Truth beyond all doubt. Amen.

TUESDAY, FORTY-FIRST WEEK   Acts 8: 14-24.

Only the Spirit of Christ Jesus within us can operate the gifts of the Holy Spirit effectively. When Simon the Magician in Samaria saw that the Holy Spirit was given through the disciples' laying-on of hands after Pentecost, he eagerly wanted to buy these gifts. But Peter denounced the greedy man who only wanted to use God for his own gain. Are we tempted at times to want God only for what He can give us and not for Himself alone? Simon missed the whole point. Peter had gone the way of the Cross and he knew that the gifts of the Spirit could not be bought with silver. They can be bought at a price, yes, but the price is *total commitment* to the Lord Jesus Christ!

Lord, let me not be trapped by the devil into seeking the gifts more than the Giver. Let my faith always be in You and not in the human instrument You use. Amen.

WEDNESDAY, FORTY-FIRST WEEK   Romans 8: 14-17.
The gift of faith sets us free from a lifetime of fear. The children of God are those moved by His Holy Spirit, not by old habit patterns. He gives us the right to cry "Abba! Father!" and *believe* that our Father hears and answers the needs of His children according to what is best for us. We are heirs of the King, children of God, and fellow heirs with Jesus! We may have to share in part of His suffering now if we are persecuted for our faith and witness, but we shall share later in His glory. The Lord's freedom in our spirits often works miracles in our bodies.

Jesus, keep my faith centered in You today so that I will not slip back into the old ways of bondage to fear. Amen.

THURSDAY, FORTY-FIRST WEEK   I Corinthians 12: 9.
St. Paul uses "gifts" in connection with healing, seemingly indicating that there are various aspects to healing. Some people seem to be better channels for emotional and spiritual healing or the healing of relationships; whereas others are used more in physical healing. Whichever it is, the thing we must remember is that the gifts are not our personal property but rather that we are *pipelines* the Lord can use to bring His rivers of living water to those in need. None of us has a gift that will make us "healers." The only true Healer is Jesus but He uses us as we offer ourselves to Him! He manifests *through* us *His gifts* to the one in need.

Lord Jesus make me useable as a channel of Your healing gifts today. Amen.

FRIDAY, FORTY-FIRST WEEK   I Corinthians 12: 10.
Many of us shy away from His gift and yet God often works His miracles through us. We may be considered strange by those worldly people who never think of praying to find a parking place or a lost item. Those of us who pray about *all*

the details of life throughout each day find that we live with miracles—what we used to call "coincidences," we now call "God-incidences." A woman's car refused to start, the battery appearing to be dead. She prayed and pressed the starter, but to no avail. Later she felt clear guidance to try again—and this time it started! The garage mechanic said it was a "loose connection." What made the car start the second time? Did the love of God make the connection? She was urgently needed on *His* "errand of mercy."

Father, thank You for all Your gifts and especially for the merciful care of Your children. Amen.

SATURDAY, FORTY-FIRST WEEK   St. Luke 18: 27.

A dean of a cathedral shared his experience one morning with a "coffee group" that had met to explore their faith in God's Providence. As an airplane pilot in the Navy during the war, he was flying a twin-engine plane with a full load of men returning home. Suddenly the plane sputtered and one engine went out and then the other, intermittently, which would have indicated sure disaster. The pilot prayed and asked his passengers to pray with him that they would be able to make the last 500 miles safely. During that long final flight across water, the engines continued to cut on and off but the plane didn't lose altitude until it was over the airport—when both engines cut out at once and the plane dropped neatly onto the airstrip! A coincidence? No—the pilot and the mechanic both agreed afterwards on examining the plane that only a miracle of God could have kept those engines functioning well enough for that particular type of plane to land safely!

Father, forgive me for failing to recognize and accept Your miracles in my life today. Amen.

MONDAY, FORTY-SECOND WEEK   Romans 8: 9 (NEB).
St. Paul wrote: "You are on the spiritual level, if only God's
Spirit dwells within you; and if a man does not possess the
Spirit of Christ, he is no Christian." These are hard words for
often we try to justify our friends or relatives as Christians
because of their good works. The gift of discernment is given
us not to criticize or fear others! Instead, we are to *pray* for
them! It is not our place to judge but to pray for the spirit of
Christ to possess those whose humanitarian "good works" do
not acknowledge Jesus as their author. If they can be kind
without His indwelling Spirit, how much more when possessed by Jesus?

Lord, help (name) to come to the knowledge of Your indwelling Spirit through this time of need. Amen.

TUESDAY, FORTY-SECOND WEEK   I John 4: 1-6.
How much we need the gifts of wisdom, knowledge, faith
and discernment *to know how to pray* for ourselves as well as
for others. St. John warns us to "test the spirits to see whether they are of God," for there are many false prophets today,
especially in the realm of the occult! They would lure us
away with their "fancy footwork," their insinuations that we
can become as gods. The serpent is—and has always been—the
symbol of Satan, not of Christian truth. Those who have the
discernment of the Holy Spirit will shun seances, astrology,
horoscopes, crystal balls, fortune telling. If you are in doubt
of a book, claim the Power of the Blood of Jesus over it and
ask His protection and discernment to show you where its
teachings are false. Don't poison your own mind. Be discrimi-
nating!

Jesus, I want *only Your* truth. Save me from wandering in
ignorance into Satan's subtle deceits today. Protect and
cleanse me. Fill me with Your light. Amen.

WEDNESDAY, FORTY-SECOND WEEK

I Corinthians 14: 1, 3, 24-25, 31-32.

When St. Paul urged the Corinthians to desire earnestly the spiritual gifts, he commended especially the ability to prophesy. He pointed out that the one "who prophesies speaks to men for their upbuilding and encouragement and consolation." One purpose is to edify the Church, not to divide it, as has happened in some meetings when a person has spoken aloud God's words of prophecy. Sometimes the Holy Spirit convicts outsiders who enter the church and suddenly hear within themselves God's revelation calling their attention to their hidden sins. This gives them an opportunity to repent and worship God: for then His Presence in their midst will be established. "The spirits of prophets are subject to the prophets" means that God will *not overrule our freedom of will* to force us to prophesy. But "all may learn and be encouraged" in a group when individuals take turns prophesying as the Holy Spirit reveals His Will for the group.

Holy Spirit, take away my self-consciousness, my fear of seeming foolish before others. Let my lips speak forth Your words of comfort or teaching—not only in my own devotional times but that others also may understand Your secrets. Amen.

THURSDAY, FORTY-SECOND WEEK

II Peter 2: 1; and I Samuel 28: 7-19; 31: 1-6.

We live in the age of false prophets that was predicted by this Scripture. In these later times Satan is trying to deceive even the elect. Spiritualism (spiritism) is one of these deceits. The prophecies coming from such sources are barren of any real meaning for their contact is with deceiving spirits not the Holy Spirit whom Jesus promised to send. They claim to contact the dead which is forbidden to Christians in numerous places in the Bible. Would we follow King Saul's sinful example when (separated from God) he consulted the witch of Endor leading to his own destruction? Would we follow a more modern example of one who tried to contact his dead son through seances, thus disobeying God's commands in Holy Scripture?

Jesus, protect me from Satan's temptations with Your precious Blood and keep me willing to be led only by Your Holy Spirit. Cleanse me and forgive me for any sin of disobedience in the past. Amen.

FRIDAY, FORTY-SECOND WEEK
I Timothy 4: 1-2 and Colossians 2: 8.
True prophecy is not ESP, thought transference, or any other natural or psychic gift. These actually *interfere* with the gifts of prophecy and discernment which are of the Holy Spirit. If we have a natural leaning to the occult or to the psychic realm, we need to *ask Jesus to cleanse all our past experiences and contacts in these areas by claiming the power of His Blood over them*. We need to commit specifically any psychic gifts to Him before we ask for His higher gifts. There are people who are like radar, picking up thought projections and "psychic disturbances" in the psychical world about them — just as weather radar picks up storms in the atmosphere. A mentally disturbed person was once exorcised and prayed for so that her "psychic door was closed to any thought projections except those filtered by the Holy Spirit." After that, she no longer "saw accidents" before they happened. She could quietly meditate without the intrusion of frightening casualties over which she had no control. She could become part of the answer to problems as Jesus let her know He needed her to pray.

Jesus, cleanse anything in me of a psychic nature; wash me in Your precious Blood and set me free from Satanic intrusions and distractions that disturb my mind and lead my thoughts away from You. Amen.

SATURDAY, FORTY-SECOND WEEK

Ephesians 1: 16-18 and Acts 21: 10-14. It is true that sometimes the Holy Spirit gives us warnings so that we can pray for someone in need. That is why when we pray for Jesus to "close the psychic door," we pray also for Him "to allow only those thoughts that have been *filtered through His Holy Spirit* to enter into our guidance centers." If the Holy Spirit gives us a prophecy, then it is so that we may know *how to pray*: to be part of the *answer* to the problem, not to bog down in fear and become part of the problem! The woman previously mentioned who was delivered from the psychic intrusions is now (a year later) able better to pray for the situations God lays on her heart through the true gifts of discernment and prophecy. She is a stalwart intercessor. She keeps her "quiet time" tryst with God and throughout the day lifts needs to Him — as the Holy Spirit reveals them through the operation of the gifts of discernment and true prophecy. She now prays in *faith*, not in distraction!

Lord Jesus, let me have only the discernment and gift of prophecy of Your Holy Spirit. Tell me how to pray, when to pray and for whom to pray in the power of Your Name today. Amen.

MONDAY, FORTY-THIRD WEEK   Romans 8: 26-27.
When the Holy Spirit prays through us, He may choose to use a familiar language or a new tongue with words we do not understand intellectually. The Spirit gives utterance, but the individual still has the choice of whether to speak or not. We can praise Jesus with the intellect or praise Him in the Spirit while the intellect lies fallow. One's spirit is edified whether

or not the intellect understands. A woman, who prayed desperately for a young friend in a critical condition, asked the Lord to use all of her being for this healing. She finally realized that she was praying in a tongue — and he was healed!

Lord, pray through my spirit as You choose to release Your healing power in the world's needs today. Amen.

TUESDAY, FORTY-THIRD WEEK
I Corinthians 14: 1-2, 14, 18; and St. Luke 11: 19-20. We need to proclaim the Holy Spirit — not promote "the gift of tongues," even though it is a valid manifestation. Some have said that the gift of tongues is of the devil, and it can be an opening for the devil if *misused*. It is almost like an arithmetic equation: to whatever extent an unloving, self-righteous spirit manifests itself in those who speak in tongues, then fear and condemnation will spring up in those who are being judged for not accepting this gift. This is an unhappy fact, but when not used in love, *any* gift can be divisive! The devil tries to play one group against the other. Those who speak in tongues can easily become bound by defensiveness if they feel threatened by the criticism of those who do not accept this gift as valid. We need to recognize Scriptural authority for the validity of this gift and with open, unprejudiced minds accept whatever the Lord wants to give us. Surely our heavenly Father would not give us something evil!

Lord, remove my prejudices and fears and make me willing to praise You in any way You choose for it is Your Holy Spirit I seek to give utterance through me. Amen.

WEDNESDAY, FORTY-THIRD WEEK
I Corinthians 14: 5, 13, 15-18, 26. The purpose of interpretation of tongues is that the Church may be edified. St. Paul wrote that he spoke in tongues more

than all the rest but he urged them to pray for the power to interpret so that others might also be blessed. He said that he prayed both in tongues and with his mind: he could sing both in the spirit and with his intellect. But he pointed out that the congregation could not say "Amen" ("so be it") unless they understood what was being said. This is why St. Paul added that in the church congregation, he would rather speak five words with his mind than ten thousand in a tongue. His purpose on such an occasion was to instruct others. In verse 26 he concluded that each person could take part in a meeting, some interpreting tongues, some giving a revelation, others a hymn or an instruction, providing "all things be done for edification." We are to seek all these supernatural (higher) gifts, but love is to be our *aim* — not pride or self-righteousness!

Lord, give me each of the gifts of the Holy Spirit as You choose so that I may be used to bless others. Amen.

THURSDAY, FORTY-THIRD WEEK

Romans 12: 8 (NEB).

The gift of preaching gives new power to old words for they come forth with the freshness of the Holy Spirit to cut people's bondages to sin, the world, and the devil. After Pentecost, timid Peter (who had denied our Lord three times) was the instrument used to convert three thousand people. The gift of preaching came to an ignorant fisherman who had no manuscript to memorize. Peter's eloquence came not from seminary training but from the Holy Spirit! As we pray daily for our ministers, let us ask the Lord to anoint their preaching so that we in the congregation may be convicted, converted, and consecrated.

Lord, let Your Holy Spirit anoint each member of Your church through the gift of preaching. Amen.

FRIDAY, FORTY-THIRD WEEK   Romans 12: 7 (NEB).

There are those who have the Holy Spirit bottled up in organization — He is bound by their human rigidities. We need to set the Holy Spirit free to use the framework of *order*: to make this work for fulfillment of God's purposes, not our human ones. This is the gift of administration: to have the Holy Spirit in spontaneous power — where *He* calls the signals and we obey with joyous freedom. We can accept reversals and changes of plans because we know that He can create a way where there is no way. Work is done more effortlessly, more joyously in the power and freedom of the Holy Spirit!

Release me, Lord, from rigidity of spirit as Your Holy Spirit enables me to administer Your purposes in my home or work today. Amen.

SATURDAY, FORTY-THIRD WEEK

Ephesians 1: 15-19.

As we study the Epistles and the book of Acts, we see reference to the operation of these gifts of the Holy Spirit. To the church at Ephesus St. Paul wrote that he prayed for God to give them "a spirit of wisdom and of revelation in the knowledge of him, having the eyes of your hearts enlightened." Here we see gifts of wisdom, knowledge, discernment, and prophecy mentioned in the saint's fervent and continuous prayer for this struggling church. Don't we need these gifts today — more visibly manifested in our Christian witness? For those who reply that they would rather have "love," may we point out that St. Paul says love is to be our *aim* and that *all* the gifts are *to be used in the way of love*! We need fruit as well as gifts, it is true. But without the gifts, we shall never have the *power* of the Holy Spirit! This was the dynamic of the early Christian Church. Don't we still need our churches to be incandescent with the power of our risen, ascended and glorified Lord? How much more will our Heavenly Father bestow upon us the Gift of His Holy Spirit when we come as children, asking in confident trust that He fulfill His promises!

Lord Jesus, give me everything that is part of Your perfect Will for my life — today and always! Amen.

PART 7

Victory Through Christ

The central theme of these meditations is "Thanks be to God who gives us the victory through our Lord Jesus Christ!" Each week day our Bible reading will focus on one of God's wonderful promises of "victory." Read the passage, absorb it, think of it often throughout the day. Meditate and let the Holy Spirit guide you to apply the thoughts to your own life. Pray the daily thanksgiving prayer, affirming Christ's victory in your own heart over sin and disease, and let His victory flow into all the world through your prayers.

Bless and heal us to Your glory, Lord, that we may become capable of a "maximum vocation" to serve You. Give us grace and power to claim Your victory in each trial — not only in our own lives but to help others live victoriously to Your glory. Amen.

MONDAY, FORTY-FOURTH WEEK   2 Timothy 1: 7.

God's power is equal to our every need; therefore, we must not be ruled by timidity which keeps us from fulfilling His purpose for our lives. He has given us His Spirit to fill us with love, to transform our lives with His power adequate in all situations. He has not given us a spirit of fear — this is Satan's temptation — but rather a sound mind!

I thank You that Your Spirit of power and love and peace dwells in my mind, transforming me into a radiant channel for Your perfect Will. Amen.

TUESDAY, FORTY-FOURTH WEEK   St. Luke 18: 27.

God's Power is beyond our largest prayers: we must not whittle Him down to our puny size! We pray as if He, the Infinite, was limited by our finite powers, asking for a teacupful when He can as well give the ocean!

I thank You, God, that this day I can turn all my praying over to Your Holy Spirit to intercede through me bringing blessings greater than I can even desire for those in need of healing. Amen.

WEDNESDAY, FORTY-FOURTH WEEK
Philippians 4: 6.

Worry is a sin most Christians fail to recognize; it is the sin of failing to trust God. The trusting soul is anxious about nothing for it accepts everything in life in an attitude of prayer and praise, looking to God for the answer to each need.

I thank You, Lord, for giving me today the trust that will let me face every decision, every crisis, every testing in the sure knowledge of Your power to guide me: to bring good out of evil, by transforming my life into Your perfect Plan. Amen.

THURSDAY, FORTY-FOURTH WEEK   I Peter 5: 7.

Jesus and St. Paul both warned us not to be anxious. We must put our whole lives into God's hands. Little worries short circuit the joy and peace He wants us to experience. He cares about us, the smallest details as well as the big problems of our lives. We want "untroubled trust" in our Father who is infinitely capable of supplying all our needs.

Father, I thank You that Your infinite love and power are now entering me: I am anxious for nothing. Amen.

FRIDAY, FORTY-FOURTH WEEK   I John 4: 18.

Fear is faith in the wrong things. We give power to what we fear: attracting it to ourselves! Jesus cautioned: "Fear not," replacing the negative idea with "only believe." If we fear cancer, our faith is more in the power of the disease than in the power of God who heals in love. He is not limited to human powers. However, we can hold back the workings of His love when we project our fears instead of faith.

Thank You, God, that today Your perfect love casts out of me all fear, filling me with peace and confident trust. Amen.

SATURDAY, FORTY-FOURTH WEEK
St. John 11: 25-26.

Jesus revealed in His own death and resurrection the Good News that death is only the means of entering into a larger and more wonderful life planned for us; "whoever believes in me shall never die." Eternal life is ours for the accepting: we become alive in His nearer Presence after we cease to live in this earthly body. We shall see our loved ones again: we shall know and be known. The joy that is set before us will be greater than any known here.

Into Your hands, Lord Jesus, I commend my spirit in perfect trust. Your Peace is now filling me with calm. Amen.

MONDAY, FORTY-FIFTH WEEK   Galatians 5: 13-18.

Lust is not only physical passion, but often expresses itself as desire for power over others, as possessive love — love that crushes or binds another to oneself, seeking to dominate and rule. Possessive love, even if well-intentioned, deprives its object of the God-given right of self-determination. It is not Christian love! How many lives have been wrecked by domineering fathers, mothers, spouses or children!

God, show me where I am possessive in love. Set me free to love as You love. Amen.

TUESDAY, FORTY-FIFTH WEEK
James 3: 13-18; and Galatians 5: 20-21.

Jealousy ranks with immorality and idolatry, ahead of drunkenness in St. Paul's list of sins. Jealousy causes deep misery in homes and churches, begetting crimes of the spirit and of the flesh. When we feel that another surpasses us, we become jealous because his success wounds our pride. If we do not live in love, our jealousy shuts off God's power in our lives.

God, forgive me for being jealous when I should rejoice in others' success. I thank You that Your love now heals me. Amen.

WEDNESDAY, FORTY-FIFTH WEEK
St. Matthew 5: 7-9.

One who gossips is neither pure in heart nor merciful; he does not make peace but is rather a sower of evil: murder of the reputation is "sin of word." Amy Carmichael describes the antidote, love, as "tenderness in judgment, unwillingness to believe evil, grief if forced to do so, eagerness to believe good, joy over one recovered from any slip or fall, unselfish gladness in another's joy, sorrow in another's sorrow, readiness to do anything to help another."

Lord, forgive me for repeating things that hurt. Amen.

THURSDAY, FORTY-FIFTH WEEK   I John 4: 16.

God is love so we cannot live with hatred for any of His creation if we really live in God's Presence. If we want His abiding in us we must let His love heal our grudges, resentments, hurt feelings and irritations *now*. We must let God's love that dwells in us flow out to those whom we cannot love in our weak human love. Let us ask in faith:

"God, love this one through me." Amen.

FRIDAY, FORTY-FIFTH WEEK   Galatians 5: 19-24.

Anger, warns St. Paul, will keep us out of the Kingdom of God. Anger releases poison in our bodies, often making us sick at our stomachs or giving us headaches. We hurt ourselves most if we become angry with others. Repeated angry flareups can develop into serious illness, especially if held over a prolonged period.

God, thank You that today Your love within me keeps me from angry reactions; no matter what happens. Amen.

SATURDAY, FORTY-FIFTH WEEK   Ephesians 4: 30-32.

God has *not* given us the right to judge or avenge, but only to love the sinner. We may hate a sin but not the sinner! We must allow Christ to make us channels of His love to redeem the life of the one who is guilty. "There, but for the grace of God, go I." Because God has forgiven us, so we must forgive, helping others in kindliness and love. Jesus forgave His enemies and if we claim to follow Him we must do the same.

Jesus, I thank You that now Your forgiving love is setting me free of intolerance for those who do not agree with me or hurt me. Amen.

MONDAY, FORTY-SIXTH WEEK   Philippians 2: 3.

Thinking of ourselves, imagining scenes or conversations in which we say or do the triumphant thing, is a sort of day-dreaming born of vanity. If we look at ourselves with eyes not blinded by spiritual pride, we see no shining angels but rather creatures of self-will. We must keep our eyes on Jesus and the beauties of His grace.

God, cleanse me of vainglorious thoughts; make me beautiful within, more like You. Amen.

TUESDAY, FORTY-SIXTH WEEK   St. John 13: 3-17.

Pride is the first and last of all sins and humility is the rarest virtue. Pride in our own talents, powers or accomplishments separates us from God whom we are supposed to glorify, not ourselves. Pride tempts us to depend on self instead of trusting in God's power. Pride makes us feel superior to others. Because Jesus washed the disciples' feet, we should be willing to do likewise.

God, I thank You that today You are setting me free from stiff-necked pride and self-worship. In true humility I now glorify You, Father. Amen.

WEDNESDAY, FORTY-SIXTH WEEK
St. Matthew 6: 24; 11: 28-30.

The world is too busy to give God His due. We need to seek solitude ("all who labor and are heavy laden") that we may rest in Him and be made new. We need perspective from the rush of life to evaluate which things are of God and which of mammon. When we have much to do, we need even *more* time to pray!

Lord, if I lose sight of You today in the pressure of many duties, remind me to look up to You and claim Your power to bring me into quiet rest in Your Presence. Amen.

THURSDAY, FORTY-SIXTH WEEK   Psalm 19: 12-14.
God sees the secret desires of our hearts, the inner cherished
ambitions that often we ourselves do not recognize. Daily, we
must ask Him to show us anything He wishes to put right for
we are often too blind to see our sins. We see the mote in our
brother's eye but not the beam in our own! If God shows us
a wrong, we must face it in His love and His forgiveness and
grace will help us correct it.

Lord Jesus, open my spiritual eyes that I may see myself as
You see me. Cleanse me and heal me; make me ready to become the temple of Your Holy Spirit. Amen.

FRIDAY, FORTY-SIXTH WEEK   I Corinthians 15: 10.
A critical spirit is so corroding it seems to be reflected in our
bodily health: arthritis has been healed as thanksgiving re-
placed critical attitudes. Rigidity of mind and spirit is linked
with rigidity of body. Remembering how much we owe to
God's grace, we sin if we condemn others self-righteously.

Lord, show me today where I am critical in spirit. Give me
Your love for all I find hard to love. Amen.

SATURDAY, FORTY-SIXTH WEEK   I Corinthians 13: 4.
Impatience is a sin that hurts us as much as it does the other
party; fretting wears out our nerves more than hard work
does. We need to develop the fruit of the Holy Spirit—
patience, awaiting the blessing promised in answer to prayer.
Often we cancel out our prayers with our impatience. Because we do not see results at once, we stop praying; we start
thinking negatively instead of waiting to see what God does.

Lord, help me to take my impatient hands off the problem.
Give me patience to let You solve it. Amen.

MONDAY, FORTY-SEVENTH WEEK   Galatians 5: 24-26.

God gives us His Holy Spirit at baptism and confirmation. At Holy Communion Christ comes into us under the forms of the bread and wine. Why, then, are we often filled with self-pity? A "martyr complex" only attracts more about which we can feel sorry for ourselves!

Thank You, Lord, for showing me now my self-pity. Help me to dethrone self and enthrone You. Amen.

TUESDAY, FORTY-SEVENTH WEEK   I John 2: 3-6.

When we are "in Christ" we are not lonely, for His Presence in us is a very real companion. He rejoices in our joys and strengthens us in our sorrows or testings. We are walking with Him every day and in His service we are drawn miraculously to rich experiences with others. He wants us to love. Why are so many lonely? It is because they have never sought Christ first; or because their own self-pity blinds them so they do not see Him standing at the door, knocking, waiting to be received in abiding love.

Lord, enter my heart to dwell now and always. Amen.

WEDNESDAY, FORTY-SEVENTH WEEK
Romans 5: 6-11.

Jesus has already achieved for us what none of us can do. On the first Good Friday He died for us so that His power might dwell in us to overcome our sin. All we have to do now is to accept His gift of reconciliation in thanksgiving and live by faith in Him, His love in us. We were doomed to break God's laws: but now, because of His death, we are released from our old carnal nature to become a new person in Christ, healed by His stripes.

Jesus, thank You that Your sacrifice enables me to be a child of God. Amen.

THURSDAY, FORTY-SEVENTH WEEK

Romans 8: 18-25.

The world is still God's world: He who created it still sustains it. Unrighteous kingdoms of the world have come and gone; but God has never been defeated. Christians need not feel futility, for the Spirit of God is moving all over the world.

God, I thank You that Your promise to come again in glory steadies me today in the midst of temptation to fear. Amen.

FRIDAY, FORTY-SEVENTH WEEK   St. Luke 18: 35-43.

The blind beggar was healed because he was alert for healing, not wallowing in self-pity. He would not be put off by those who tried to discourage him. He knew his need and stated it positively. He did not whine out a long list of details, an "organ recital." Many are not healed today because they enjoy the attentions paid to their illness—(they want pity more than healing); others, because they fear the responsibilities of being well.

God, deliver me from self-pity that holds back Your healing power. Amen.

SATURDAY, FORTY-SEVENTH WEEK

St. John 14: 1-3.

Death is a doorway into the Larger Life, the nearer Presence of God. The veil separating us from our relatives in the communion of saints is at times lifted by God's mercy when we feel their loving nearness. Though we are not to contact them, we can still help, releasing them in our thoughts and prayers into the joy of the Lord! We must not hold them back in our grief; we miss them now but we shall be reunited later.

Thank You, God, that in Your love we are one with loved ones in Your Heavenly Kingdom. Your peace and joy now fill the loneliness. Amen.

MONDAY, FORTY-EIGHTH WEEK   St. John 16: 20.

Our Lord is most real to us in our sorrow. When no human being can comfort us, He draws us nearer to His great heart of Love. We need not remain in the well, for from it He enables us to draw strength: from the "depths of divine streams" we drink the water of life, His new life given for us. Through sorrow we learn how to lose our dependence on the shallow joys of the world and hold onto His things that are eternal!

Thank You, God, that today Your divine love is flooding me. Amen.

TUESDAY, FORTY-EIGHTH WEEK   St. Luke 9: 48.

God has a purpose for each of us. Jesus said that we receive Him when we receive one of His children. Each of us is known to God, our Father. We are created as individuals, each with his own fingerprint, no two alike. Surely God has as much a plan for His creation as an architect has for his building or the ship designer for his ship! We have only to pray to find God's plan, but we must be willing to *obey* if it is to become effective in our lives!

Lord, Your Plan is better than mine. I give You my life that You may unfold it, beginning now. Amen.

WEDNESDAY, FORTY-EIGHTH WEEK   St. John 14: 27.

Jesus promised us His peace. Why, then, are we creatures of tension? Do we claim His peace in a "quiet time" of prayer each morning? Do we waste His time and ours with petty worries? Do we look constantly to Him throughout the day for strength, affirming His peace?

Blot out tension in my "prayer tryst" that I may wait upon You today. Amen.

THURSDAY, FORTY-EIGHTH WEEK   Psalm 46.

How often dread of this or that event or decision robs us of inner joy and peace, paralyzing constructive thought or action. Often we dread to meet this person or that situation because we feel inadequate. One dread seems to beget others till sometimes we feel we must run from life. Alcohol, pills or frivolities can become props or escapes, but are, alas, *false security*! We need dread nothing but the loss of God's Presence: with Him, by the power of His Name, we are given needed strength.

Thank You, God, for the assurance that I can face anything in Your power with expectancy of Your peace now. Amen.

FRIDAY, FORTY-EIGHTH WEEK   Romans 8: 28-30.

Why do we so often despair when God has promised that nothing happens to us without His caring? If we and our loved ones are in God's hands we have no need to despair, even if things seem desperate! He can bring good out of evil, making it serve His merciful plans.

God, I thank You that my despair is now being transformed into Your peace. Amen.

SATURDAY, FORTY-EIGHTH WEEK   Psalm 103.

"Mental illness" or uncontrollable depression is often "soul sickness." God is the remedy; not tranquilizers. Psychoanalysis helps identify a problem but does not always solve it. If the details of one's past—like the works of a fine watch—are spread out on the table, who will repair and put things right again? Only God who created us can forgive sins. To excuse sin "because everyone does it" will not help.

God, forgive me, I have sinned; restore me to Your peace. Amen.

MONDAY, FORTY-NINTH WEEK
St. Matthew 10: 37-39.
Shyness is really self-consciousness, much as we dislike to admit it. Shy people have been transformed by a conversion experience that makes Jesus the center of their lives. Where once they thought, "What do people think of me?" now they think, "What do people think of Christ?"

Jesus, let me die unto self that I may be risen with You to new life. Amen.

TUESDAY, FORTY-NINTH WEEK   2 Corinthians 3: 5.
We have been taught that "God helps all who help themselves." True, but this does not mean we are to be *self*-sufficient. Our sufficiency is of God! We are to help ourselves but not put our trust in our own wisdom, strength, talents alone! We are to use the gifts and powers which He has given us in a spirit of thankful stewardship and dependence on Him.

Lord, let me never think I have wisdom enough without You or talents enough without Your Grace. I can do nothing well of myself alone: I am adequate because I trust in You. Amen.

WEDNESDAY, FORTY-NINTH WEEK
Colossians 1: 9-14.
As Christians we are to set our affections on the higher things of life. How little account are some of the hurts we have allowed to become imbedded, rankling in our hearts and poisoning our bodies! A doctor told a patient: "Either you must cut out your resentments or I shall have to cut out part of your intestines." The man set right his longstanding differences with a former business partner and never had to have the operation!

God, free me from pettiness that I may be healed. Amen.

THURSDAY, FORTY-NINTH WEEK

2 Corinthians 9: 6-15.

Do we give back to God His due of what He has given to us?
The widow's mite was in proportion to her means; is our
giving in proportion to our blessings or is it an insult to God?
Do we give to the church because *we need* to express our
thanks to God? Or do we give only what we think we can
"get by with?"

Forgive my past ingratitude, Lord. I give now to Your work,
cheerfully and gratefully. Amen.

FRIDAY, FORTY-NINTH WEEK   St. Matthew 7: 21.

Wishful thinking, "leaving it to John," will never bring in the
Kingdom of God. We need to pray daily. "Here am I Lord:
send me." But when He prompts us to visit some lonely or
sick person, let us not deny His Holy Spirit. We would not be
Christians today if others had been as lazy as we. A missionary field lies all about us.

I shall give thanks by taking the Good News of Your healing
love to one You show me today, God. Use me as Your channel, Lord. Amen.

SATURDAY, FORTY-NINTH WEEK

Revelation 3: 15-22.

Are we asking Christ to heal us when we are indifferent to
the needs of others and to His work of bringing His Kingdom
on earth? He knocks: and waits for us to respond. Will we be
judged like the church at Laodicea as being lukewarm? Or are
we on fire in our faith? We can share the healing mercies of
our Lord Jesus Christ or we can share in the indifference of
the world. We do not shape Christ to our own liking. He
stands before us, confronting us with His demand to *love*!

Lord, forgive my indifference to needs of others. Heal them
through me. Amen.

MONDAY, FIFTIETH WEEK   St. Matthew 25: 1-13.

Procrastination is different from "waiting upon the Lord." If we are in doubt of God's Will, it is wise to test our inward impulse with the Bible! What would Jesus do? When we are sincerely praying for guidance, God usually allows circumstances to arrange themselves pointing the way to discern His Will. When impulse, Holy Scripture and circumstances are in agreement, we may move one step at a time praying for continued guidance.

God, let me not delay Your Plan. Amen.

TUESDAY, FIFTIETH WEEK   Romans 15: 1-6.

Disobedience is not merely breaking God's commandments: it is also failing to seek constant growth in our devotion to Him! How often we see the attitude: "I'm a good Christian; I don't hurt anyone and I mind my own business." Is this Christ's attitude to us? There has been too much withholding from God: His call is to *share His blessings* to enrich the world.

God, I thank You that You know what I am capable of doing. When You call me today, give me the grace to obey. Amen.

WEDNESDAY, FIFTIETH WEEK   1 John 1:6; 2:6.

When guilty, we often point a finger at someone else to take our eyes off our own sins. Psychiatrists say we criticize in others the very things we dislike in ourselves. We are irritated because we are reminded of our weakness. Our guilt can be wiped out only by God in answer to the prayer of repentance. He always answers our pleas for forgiveness when we are truly contrite, willing to make restitution, like the prodigal son—but not when we are only sorry to be ill!

Lord, I have sinned; I am not worthy of Your death on the Cross for me. Forgive me. Amen.

THURSDAY, FIFTIETH WEEK   James 5: 12-18.

When we have sinned and have not repented, we feel it necessary to justify ourselves. We cite the conduct of others but only Jesus' conduct is a valid standard. Instead of making excuses we need to face our sin squarely, wanting to be set free from it, willing to do whatever God tells us. For those whose consciences cannot be quieted, it is often helpful to confess to God in the presence of a priest who then pronounces in God's Name *His* words of forgiveness.

Lord, I believe, I repent. By faith I am now justified, forgiven, at peace. Amen.

FRIDAY, FIFTIETH WEEK
St. Mark 11: 22-26; and Hebrews 11: 1-3.

Lack of expectancy in prayer is disobedience because Jesus said we were to believe we *had* received; and *then we would receive.* "Faith is the assurance of things hoped for." Why don't we give God expectancy, the substance of real faith, from which the desired blessing will come? We are like the woman who prayed one night for a mountain to be removed, and then said the next day, "I knew it wouldn't happen!"

Lord, make us expectant that our "mountains" will be removed in Your way and time. Amen.

SATURDAY, FIFTIETH WEEK   Colossians 3: 1-11.

If we depend on the world's "other gods" we shall have their weakness instead of God's strength for we shall disobey the first commandment. Dependence on God sets us free from reliance on wealth, prestige, vain pleasures, sedatives, stimulants, etc. Healing of our bodies must wait often for healing of our loyalties.

God, loose me from bondage to worldly values. I now humbly put on Your love. Amen.

MONDAY, FIFTY-FIRST WEEK   St. Matthew 11: 29-30.

Pain responds to the prayer of faith. Nurses have asked "What is it?" after seeing a praying patient endure a serious operation relatively free of pain. Even terminal diseases seem not to cause extreme pain in those who are prayed for. We thank God for anesthetists and doctors who spare patients unnecessary pain. But we can pray for release when burned by cooking oil or bitten by insects or subjected to the dentist's drill.

Thank You, God, Your Will is not suffering; Your healing is now relieving me of bodily pain. Amen.

TUESDAY, FIFTY-FIRST WEEK   Ephesians 1: 3-14.

God does not *intentionally* will so many things we glibly attribute to Him, but He has *allowed us freedom of will*. When told piously that her father's death in a plane crash was "God's Will," a six-year-old replied, "Then I hate God!" How dare we accuse God of willing such a thing! A mechanic's sloppy work, a pilot's faulty judgment, an irresponsible pilot off course may be the cause of such a tragedy. Jesus proved God's Will is to heal and bless!

God, forgive us for blaming You when humans err or sin, causing accidents. Release Your Power to bring good. Amen.

WEDNESDAY, FIFTY-FIRST WEEK
St. Mark 5: 24-34; and St. Matthew 13: 58.

Jesus healed all who came to Him. Only in Nazareth was He unable to do His mighty works of healing—because of the unbelief of the people there. We today are too like Nazareth. His commission to heal has been left out of too many churches; but it is still valid!

Jesus, I thank You that Your touch still has its ancient power. I come in faith to be healed by You. Amen.